Changing Legacies:
Growing Up In An Alcoholic Home

Published by: Health Communications, Inc.
2119-A Hollywood Boulevard
Hollywood, FL 33020

Printed in the United States of America.

First printing, soft cover.
ISBN: 0-932194-20-6

TABLE OF CONTENTS

Psycho-Social Stages of Development in
Adult Children of Alcoholics
By Kay Brooks 1
Pre-School-Aged Children from Alcoholic Families
By Stella Nicholson 7
Prevention, Intervention & Treatment for Grade-School-
Aged Children of Alcoholics
By Barbara Naiditch 13
Insight to the Oldest Child from An Alcoholic Family
By Cardwell C. Nuckols 19
Planning Community-Based Services for Children
From Alcoholic Families
By Claudia Black 25
Community Prevention: Creating Choices For Children
From Alcoholic Families
By Charles Deutsch 33
Conflict and Crisis Typify Life for Children
From Alcoholic Families
By Rebecca Black 37
The Family Law in Alcoholic Homes—Don't Talk
By Claudia Black 39
Understanding and Helping Children of Alcoholics
By Charles Deutsch 43
School-Based Intervention Strategies for Children
From Alcoholic Families
By Rokelle Lerner 53
Inadequate, Inconsistent ... Non-Existent Parenting:
A Dilemma for Children From Alcoholic Families
By Tom Perrin 57
Emotional Caretaking, Parental Roles & Self-Esteem:
Three Personal Stories
By Jael Greenleaf 65
Children of Alcoholics: The Clinical Profile
By Claudia Black 73
Common Characteristics of Adult Children
From Alcoholic Families
By Janet Woititz 77
Alcoholic Parents: Reducing the Impact
By Robert J. Ackerman 89

Psycho-Social Stages of Development in Adult Children of Alcoholics

By Kay F. Brooks

"I felt like I had a plastic shield between me and the world. I could see everyone and even talk and physically touch them. But the plastic shield was always there to protect me."
Anonymous adult child of alcoholic, age 24.

The psychosocial development of adult children of chemically-dependent (CD) systems will be examined within the framework of the eight stages of such development, as understood by E.H. Erickson. Erickson's stages of development are an extension of Freud's description of the stages of development through which a child passes, with the first four stages dominated by unconscious drives, and the last four dominated by conscious thought processes.

There are two imporant factors to keep in mind regarding Erickson's stages. First, in each of the stages of development there are critical periods through which the individual must pass. As illustrated in the chart on Page 4, success or failure at these critical points produces differing impacts on the individual's personality. Failure at any one of these stages jeopardizes full development at the later stages. Secondly, the individual's personality is always in a state of evolution and open to change, both forward and backward through the stages. Thus, it is important not to make the assumption, for instance, that Trust or Intimacy is an achievement, secured once and for all, at a given state. As an individual finds the self unable to cope with present circumstances, regression can occur.

1

It readily can be seen that a child born into a chemically dependent family system, which is experiencing emotional, cognitive and behavioral dysfunction, would immediately have difficulty with the first stage of development. In many cases, a child in such a home experiences abuse, and, particularly if the mother is the CD, neglect. As events and adults are unconsciously perceived to be, at the very least, inconsistent, if not overtly harmful, the child will sense the dis-ease in the environment, and will not be able to find that psychological sense of security and safety, that surety of psychological position defined as Trust. Instead, this child will develop a sense of Mistrust that it will carry for the rest of its life, unless it receives the opportunity to address this issue through therapy or a recovery program.

For the child whose home environment is not affected by chemical dependency at this stage of development, Trust can develop, providing the base for the next stage. This child will have learned to have a basic trust in individuals and will interact with others in a trusting and open fashion. This pattern of behavior will continue as long as it is rewarded by others. If, however, at some time during the individual's life, the trusting behavior is consistently responded to with rejection or hostility by others, such as that manifested by a family system in middle or late stages of chemical dependency, or if this child marries a CD, the trusting behavior will begin to disappear. In such a circumstance, it can be said that the individual loses the ability to behave in a trusting fashion. Such a movement is part of the evolution through the stages, and represents regression.

In the Later Infancy Stage, the successful passing through the second stage of development forms the foundation on which the child can separate self from the family system. The Autonomy achieved by this separation is vital in coping with the CD family system, the nature of which is to enmesh its members into the problem. For the child who passes successfully through this second stage of development, only to later meet up with persons who send the message that the individual is not worthy of respect, or is inadequate, regression may occur. In that case, the individual will have lost Autonomy and now have Shame and Doubt about self.

Without Autonomy, a child will absorb the family dis-ease, and internalize at the unconscious level the message that, "If something is wrong, **then I am wrong.**" Any child whose family system has no chemical dependency at this stage, or is in early stages of the disease, may be able to develop the necessary Autonomy to separate self from the later dysfunction and maintain a sense of identity when the disease is in the late stage. But the child who spends these early years in a severely distressed family system is rarely provided that necessary respect by parents, or is taught self-control. In most cases, this child sees adults who are not showing respect for each other, let alone for the child. The child also sees adults who have obvious lack of self-control of both emotions and behavior. The end result is that this child, on top of Mistrust from the previous stage of development, now views self with Shame and Doubt. For how can I feel good about myself if I feel bad about what is going on around me, and I **am** what is going on around me—I have no Autonomy. If my environment is shameful, then I am shameful. And thus, the child doubts the worth of self.

The Early Childhood Stage, which encourages the testing of reality on the part of the child, is obviously one in which a child of a middle or late-stage CD family will have difficulty. One of the dilemmas for a child in such a home is that of often being told that what one sees is not real, that something really didn't happen, that it wasn't "that bad." In fact, rather than being encouraged to develop the imagination as the appropriate psychological task, a child may even be told that what it thought it heard or saw was only its imagination. Thus, this important task for this stage is thwarted. Often, the child is made to feel guilty about talking about what they are experiencing, and the line between reality and imagination becomes blurred. Even when the child doesn't talk about reality, it will struggle to maintain a sense of reality, regardless of what denial is being perpetrated within the family system. Therefore, this child will even feel guilty for having, unstated though it is, a different perception than other family members. This increases the child's self-doubt, because it cannot totally trust its own sense of reality. It will be hard for this child to develop Initiative, because it will feel guilty about setting goals based upon its own reality. This child may become locked into being a follower, letting others exercise their imaginations, and letting others define reality.

The Middle Childhood Stage presents a way of viewing those "Hero" or "Responsible" children of the CD family who have developed Industry, who have a sense of duty or accomplishment. Such children frequently are the oldest, chldren who may have successfully passed through the previous stages before the family disease was present, or was only in the early stages and did not hinder successful passages. However, if family distress becomes severe enough when the child reaches this stage, successful passage may stop. Thus, the child becomes locked into performance and accomplishment, and is unable to move to the next stage successfully—the stage where it can determine what it can, and more importantly for this child, what it **cannot** do. A child who cannot pass from this stage of Industry will have difficulty realizing its own limitations, and therefore will have difficulty with the Ego-Identity Stage.

ERICKSON'S PSYCHOSOCIAL STAGES OF DEVELOPMENT

SUCCESS		FAILURE
I. EARLY INFANCY (Birth to 1 Year)		
TRUST: Child receives affection and needed satisfaction.	VS	**MISTRUST:** Child abused or neglected.
II. LATER INFANCY (1-3 Years)		
AUTONOMY: Child encouraged to develop self-control and is provided respect by parents.	VS	**SHAME AND DOUBT:** Child made to feel inadequate and not worthy of respect.
III. EARLY CHILDHOOD (4-5 Years)		
INITIATIVE: Child encouraged to use imagination and test reality on own.	VS	**GUILT:** Child made to feel guilty about fantasies. Reality testing is is discouraged.
IV. MIDDLE CHILDHOOD (6-11 Years)		
INDUSTRY: Child has developed sense of duty and accomplishment.	VS	**INFERIORITY:** Child does not value accomplishment. Exhibits sense of failure.
V. PUBERTY AND ADOLESCENCE (12-20 Years)		
EGO IDENTITY: Individual has now developed a sense of self-concept, a sense of what they are not, can do, cannot do.	VS	**ROLE CONFUSION:** Individual has no real sense of being. Confused about self and relation to world.
VI. EARLY ADULTHOOD		
INTIMACY: Individual has ability to form close relationships.	VS	**ISOLATION:** Individual remains apart from others, may even be antagonistic toward them.
VII. MIDDLE ADULTHOOD		
GENERATIVITY: Time of productivity in work and family.	VS	**STAGNATION:** Time of non-productivity and wandering. No real accomplishments in any area.
VIII. LATE ADULTHOOD		
INTEGRITY: Approaches state of self-actualization.	VS	**DESPAIR:** Loss of faith in self and others. Fearful of approaching death.

For the child who cannot develop Industry during the Middle Childhood Stage, the result will be a feeling of Inferiority. Two factors may lead to this: (1) If all passages before have been unsuccessful, this child will arrive at Middle childhood with a sense of Mistrust, Shame/Doubt and Guilt. With such a psychological self-concept, Inferiority is predictable; (2) another reason may be that this is a younger child, one who arrived as the CD family system was more dysfunctional than that experienced by the older child at this stage. While that older child could achieve Industry, based upon successful passages, this younger child cannot compete with the achieving child, and therefore, will have a sense of Inferiority.

By the time a child reaches the next stage, Puberty and Adolescence, one needs all the successes of the previous stages to cope with the turmoils and mysteries of this period. For the child who has failed at the previous stages, and arrives at this stage with Inferiority, role confusion is inevitable. This child is truly unable to have a sense of self, because the self is unacceptable, e.g., nontrusting, shameful, self-doubting, guilty, as well as inferior. Also, the encroaching effects upon the self of the CD system will chip away at the sense-of-self. In addition, a child who reaches this stage of development at a time when the family system itself is experiencing role confusion, even role reversal of husband/male and wife/female roles, due to the inability of the CD person to fulfill his/her role, a child does not have role models as references. In a family system where children are often called upon to participate in adult fights, rescue-behavior, caretaking, etc., how does a child know what roles are, or how they are defined? In many cases, little distinction is made betwen adults and children, especially if the spouse turns to the children to fulfill unmet intimacy needs which should appropriately be met at the adult level. With all this role confusion, a result is often that young boys become "little men," and young women stay "little girls," roles they continue to play far into adulthood. Or the reverse is true. Men stay "little boys," and young girls assume the role of "mother."

Passing successfully through the Young Adult Stage and achieving the ability for Intimacy is nearly impossible for the child who arrives at this stage with Mistrust, Shame/Doubt, Guilt, Inferiority, and Role Confusion. And yet, this child will be desperate for Intimacy, as a way of getting out of the Isolation. It

5

seems to make sense, within this view of Erickson's stages of development, that this child may initially feel intimate and even "at home" with another person who has been involved in a CD family system. This will not be a personal, psychological intimacy, but rather a "fitting with" another dysfunctional system, or another person who also has been unable to pass successfully through the developmental stages. Like water seeking its own level, these adult children will find each other, whether they partner with a CD, with another adult child of a CD family system, or with a child of some other kind of severely-dysfunctional family system. If one partner is a CD and the other is that older child who has had some success at passage through the stages, that older child will not begin to have difficulty in continued, successful passage, and will probably begin regression, as the disease of the partner begins to move into the individual's psychology. In fact, the CD may begin to show that antagonism so common of those in Isolation, and begin to attack the Ego Identity, Industry, Initiative and Autonomy of the older child-partner, who is accused of being "so good, so perfect, so superior." Thus, even though this older child may have escaped the negative self-views in the earlier passages, this child, as an adult, will develop in the backwards evolution of the stages, all of the Mistrust, Shame/Doubt, Guilt, Inferiority, Role Confusion and Isolation, as if the successful passages had never been made.

For those adult children of CD family systems who do not partner with a CD, but find each other, they will be unable to establish Intimacy, and will end up journeying together (if they stay together), through Middle Adulthood, each alone and in Isolation within the partnership. They will arrive side-by-side at the same point in time: the Despair of Late Adulthood, aptly named, for to have spent a lifetime feeling Mistrust, Shame/Doubt, Guilt, Inferiority, Role Confusion, Isolation and Stagnation is indeed Despair!

For those who care about the particular needs of adult children of CD family systems, this information on the psychosocial stages of development can point the direction for therapy and healing. For each adult child must begin again the passage through the stages of successful personality development, beginning with Trust issues. The author's own personal work with such adult children has shown repeatedly that the focus must come back to the Trust issue, whether it be with the therapist, a support group, a recovery group, or, and perhaps especially, with the god of that adult child's understanding.

Pre-School Aged Children From Alcoholic Families

By Stella M. Nicholson

For years, professionals in the field of chemical dependency have been providing services for individuals who are addicted. There has been tremendous progress made with regard to elevating the chemically dependent's "bottom." Many addicts seen today within mental health facilities, crisis centers and outpatient services are not in late stages of addiction, thanks to the efforts of the media, prominent figures in politics, sports, performing arts, music, and other professionals who have dedicated their energies to enlightening others at a national level, by sharing their own personal addiction experiences. Destigmatization of chemical dependency has become more of a reality.

Unfortunately, until recently, family members were not getting too much notoriety. Their "bottoms" have not been as elevated as the chemically dependents'. The little attention that was given to the family members' recovery was directed at the spouse or teenage members through programs such as Al-Anon, Alateen and Families Anonymous. Children under the age of 12 received the least attention of all. The issues of the drinking parents and the effects upon this age group were largely ignored by those working in the field of addiction. For this group, the stigma remained.

These youngsters were on an island with their feelings. Whereas adults and teens could converse and share "their experiences, strength and hope," these children seemed to have no one to talk to, nowhere to go, and no "adult" method to communicate. Children under the age of 12 receive little of the attention they so desperately need.

Oftentimes I've heard statements such as, "The children are so young, I'm sure they didn't know what was going on with their father," or "Well, Bill goes to A.A., I go to Al-Anon, and our older children are going to Alateen, but our two youngest ... well, we get a baby sitter for them." Isolation from the family for these children can be just as acute after recovery as it was prior to it. Under the umbrella of "protection for their own good," or "they don't understand what's going on," these children were left out of the "what it was like, what happened, and what it is like now" stages of addiction and recovery.

In working with pre-schoolers, I can assure you that they are aware of what is going on within their family systems. All you have to do is ask them and they will, without reservation, describe what is going on inside and outside their homes.

The children with whom I work display a variety of behaviors, from aggression to passivity. There are two major forms o acting-out behavior—first, the overt behavior, and secondly, the covert behavior.

Children who display overt behavior will test boundaries, rules and you. They are testing to see if people will still find them to be loveable in spite of their inappropriate behavior. If they are rejected, a self-fulfilling prophecy of "I am unloveable" emerges.

The children who display covert behavior, typically by withdrawal, tend to internalize all of their feelings. These children have found that being passive works best for them. Passive children do not "make waves." Therefore, they go through life not getting very much attention. If someone was observing their non-verbal behavior, they often appear as if they are about to disappear inside their own bodies.

There are several techniques that can be utilized to help pre-schoolers from chemically dependent homes. Briefly listed below are just a few which I have found to be effective in helping these children to discuss their feelings; to develop coping skills which are more appropriate than the ones which they are currently using; and more importantly, to help them to develop a greater sense of self-esteem and self-worth. I have used these techniques in groups of 3-10 children, or during individual counseling.

1. Provide them with a nurturing and safe environment. Tell them often that whatever they tell you will not be shared with anyone.

2. Regress in the best interests of the children. Enter their world of reality by actively participating in the activity upon which you have decided. If you decide to play "animal games," then get on the floor yourself and participate with them. Feelings that are often hidden can come out in an aggressive lion, angry tiger, or cuddly puppy dog. In the beginning of therapy, this will help you earn their trust.

3. Educate them about alcoholism or drug addiction by utilizing films and other written material geared toward this population, e.g., *"Lots of Kids Like Us,"* a film produced by Gerald Rogers Productions; the workbook, *"My Dad Loves Me, My Dad Has A Disease,"* by Claudia Black, etc.

4. Encourage them to share their experiences with the group with regard to their parents' drinking or drug use. They may refer to the chemically dependent person as having the "sickness." Puppets are helpful in getting kids to talk about these issues.

5. Utilize stem sentences to motivate them to talk, e.g., "When my dad drinks, I feel ... ," "When I'm angry, I ... ," "Sometimes I want to hurt ..." Write these incomplete sentences out, place them in a plastic bag, and allow the children to pick out what they chose to. Read it to them, let them respond, and move on to the next child.

6. Have story-telling sessions that problem-solve various situations, e.g., "Homer the Homely Hound Dog;" "Alexander and the Terrible, Horrible, No Good, Very Bad Day;" "The Family that Changed," etc.

These techniques have motivated children to change their behavior. The children spend the first half-hour of the session doing artwork. I have found children who have difficulty in

9

expressing their feelings can accomplish and overcome that problematic area by drawing their feelings. After they have completed their drawings, they are requested to identify what the picture means to them. It's important to be directive when you are trying to identify specific feelings. I also give them the opportunity to draw whatever they wish to hang on the bulletin board, or to take home with them.

In conclusion, it is my theory that providing services for young children, beginning with pre-schoolers, can reduce the possible risk of their either becoming chemically dependent or marrying someone who is chemically dependent. If, at an early age, children can learn how to deal with their feelings, examine their alternatives, cope with their environment, and learn that there are family systems that operate differently from the ones in which they live, perhaps these children can impact upon the next generation. The late Karen Carpenter's song, *"Blessed are the Beasts and the Children,"* beautifully tells others that children have rights and need to be treated with the same dignity and respect that adults wish to have in their own lives. I invite those of you who can provide services for these children to make that commitment to yourself and to them. Perhaps with your assistance, together we can impact upon our greatest human resources ... our children of tomorrow.

The pre-school children with whom I work demonstrate identifiable roles which I call adaptive type, little adult type, rebel type, and disciplinarian type. The adaptive type complies with everyone, people-pleases, and goes along with whatever you want them to do. The little adult type is extremely responsible, always wants to help out, has all the right answers and problem-solves for the other children. The rebel type acts out often, is disruptive, interrupts everyone and bullies other children. The disciplinarian orders, advises, and attempts to straighten everyone out.

These children utilize defense mechanisms to protect themselves from their environment. It is not unusual to observe regression, emotional insulation, denial, repression and acting out defenses. They are attempting to cope with their environment the only way they psychologically can. These children do not know how healthy families operate, because they have not been exposed to anything outside of their own system.

Developmental theorists, child psychiatrists and psychologists, social workers, and early childhood educators have stated that the first five years of life are the most crucial. Dr. Thomas Verney, in his book, *"The Secret Life of the Unborn Child,"* believes that crucial years begin *in utero*. Dr. Robert Ackerman, in his book, *"Children of Alcoholics,"* has dedicated a chapter which interfaces alcoholism with Eric Erickson's psycho-social stages of development. Claudia Black's workbook for children, *"My Dad Loves Me, My Dad Has A Disease,"* utilizes drawings from some of the children with whom she has worked as a method by which to explain alcoholism and its symptomology to children. Her workbook contains relevant materials geared toward helping children understand that they are not alone in their feelings or experiences.

It is my belief that professionals in the field of chemical dependency, early childhood educators, pre-school teachers, and school counselors need to develop a systematic approach to provide services for pre-schoolers. Pre-schoolers grow into adults and, without proper intervention, will perpetuate the family system with which they are most familiar, or become chemically dependent themselves. The statistics clearly state that over 50% of the recovering alcoholics who participate in Alcoholics Anonymous have an alcoholic parent; 40% of the individuals involved in Al-Anon also had an alcoholic parent, and most of this number proceeded to marry an alcoholic. Currently, there are an estimated 28 million children who are affected by alcoholism or drug dependency.

Prevention, Intervention and Treatment for Grade School-Aged Children of Alcoholics

By Barbara Naiditch

Children aged 5-12 from chemically dependent family systems are the most underserved population today. There are very few programs nationwide that provide services to this age population. There are very few training programs that train individuals how to develop children's programming, how to intervene, or how to develop treatment programs for this high-risk population

According to the National Association for Children of Alcoholics (which was formed in February, 1983), children of alcoholics have an adjustment reaction to familial alcoholism which is a recognizable, diagnosable, and treatable condition—variously referred to as co-dependency, co-alcoholism, or para-alcoholism. Despite the widespread recognition and acceptance of alcoholism as a family illness, children of alcoholics continue to be ignored, undiagnosed, and untreated.

There are an estimated 28-35 million Americans who have at least one alcoholic parent. Four to six children out of every 25 in any given classroom come for alcoholic homes. Great strides have been taken in combating chemical dependency, but children of alcoholics have been left behind. No more than 5% are getting the help they need. Medical research has shown that children born to alcoholics are at the highest risk of developing attention deficit disorders, stress-related medical problems, fetal alcohol syndrome, and other alcohol-related birth defects. Children of alcoholics are prone to experience a range of psychological difficulties, including learning disabilities, anxiety, attempted and completed suicide, eating disorders, and compulsive achieving.

Chemical dependency impedes child development. Prevention, intervention, and treatment programs need to help children fill in their missing deficiencies so they can move on developmentally. These young people so often have a poor self-concept, are easily frustrated, often perform poorly in school, lack positive coping skills, and are more likely than their peers to suffer adjustment problems in adolescence. Developmentally, children from 0-5 need: consistency; positive role models; a trusting, secure environment; structure; information; and a chance to experience play.

Children 6-12 need the above, plus: opportunity for positive feed-back; positive attention from peers and adults; concrete information about alcoholism; and consistent discipline/clear boundary setting.

What can health professionals, counselors, social workers, school systems, nurses, psychologists, day care providers, Al-Anon and A.A. members, and parents do for these innocent victims?

Setting up support groups for children 5-12 years of age is crucial for prevention, intervention, and treatment of the effects of parental alcoholism. Children Are People, Inc., has been working with these young people in support groups since 1977, and has as its basic goals: developing in the child a positive self-image; providing education to children and parents about alcoholism as a family illness; teaching children to recognize personal emotions and their impact on mood and behavior; teaching children to develop satisfying choices for coping with stressful situations; building a sense of trust with the adults who are consistent role models; involving the family through intake, family communication workshops, and newsletters.

As a result of these goals, Barbara Naiditch and Rokelle Lerner created the Children Are People, Inc. Support Group Model. The main emphasis of the group is to teach children to find satisfying alternatives for coping with stress, so that they need not turn to drugs as the only alternative. Through games, discussions, poetry, music and art, children learn about feelings, defenses, chemical dependency, choices, family worth and specialness. The groups meet once weekly for eight weeks. On the eighth week, parents are invited to participate with their children in a communications workshop. This support group model has been adapted to elementary schools in 19 states. The model has also been adapted to Mental Health Centers, Youth Service Bureaus, Child Protection Teams at welfare departments and YMCA's. Support groups assist children while a family member is still using chemicals, while a member is in treatment, and during the time a family is in aftercare groups and recovery.

Why aren't there more programs that include children as part of prevention, intervention and treatment? After researching those questions for the main thrust of this article, I discovered that there are few training programs nationwide that can teach the participants to develop programs for children of alcoholics. This is a newly-emerging field. I have focused most of my efforts on children ages 5-12, and their families. There needs to be more research and training in program development for adolescent and adult children of alcoholics.

Despite the obvious need for services, there has been little action taken by those in the alcoholism field, or by relevant agencies to deal with the needs of these children. According to Charles Deutsch in his book *"Broken Bottles, Broken Dreams,"* many professionals who work in alcoholism clinics are insufficiently trained in the child's perspective.

Training seminars need to be established to: (1) Train elementary schools in development of support groups for their high-risk children; (2) Train counselors in CD treatment programs to develop elementary-age programming through lectures, family treatment involvement, or aftercare support groups; (3) train health care professionals in program development for children of alcoholics (ages 5-12); (4) train Al-Anon and A.A. members to facilitate support groups for 5-12-year-olds; and (5) train social workers, family therapists, psychologists and day care providers to develop programs for children of alcoholics.

Training programs need to address the following: (1) teach adult concepts in children's terminology; (2) teach behavior pathology of children of alcoholics; (3) teach participants different modalities of therapy that can be used with young people such as movement therapy, art therapy, play therapy and poetic therapy; (4) intervention techniques in elementary schools; (5) family illness concept of what chemical dependency is; (6) normal/dysfunctional developmental stages of children; (7) skill building in parental and child interaction; (8) creative adaptation of support group models to different cultures—Black, Native Americans, Hispanics; (9) alternative programming in prevention, intervention and treatment programs that can be adapted to individual agencies, mental health programs, treatment centers and school systems; and (1) teach support group models to participants.

During the next five years, I see an urgent need to train, motivate, and educate treatment center staffs, school systems, mental health centers, social workers, psychologists, psychiatrists and nurses to begin to be aware of the special needs of children of alcoholics.

If enough people are trained to develop programs in prevention, intervention, and treatment, perhaps young people can be provided with more choices to equip them for coping with stress, so that they need not have harmful chemicals as an only alternative. Perhaps, too, youngsters can be given an opportunity to learn to value themselves and to interact with peers to develop friendships and to heighten acceptance. Often, these young people are the forgotten age, in terms of drug and dependency issues. More funding needs to be provided to develop children's programs in all modalities of treatment. If we do nothing to intervene in the lives of children, we are promoting and enabling another generation of alcoholics.

Children Are People, Inc. has pioneered the development of support groups for children 5-12 from chemically dependent families, and has pioneered the development of training seminars to assist professionals who want to incorporate programming for children as a part of recovery.

Research conducted by Children Are People, Inc. indicates that these children are usually kept out of the treatment process, and that they are an underserved population in the continuum of care.

Children Are People, Inc. is the only agency in the country that trains persons in methods for developing, implementing and facilitating and adapting the CAP Model in schools, treatment centers, mental health centers, and community agencies. Children Are People, Inc. also trains staffs in elementary school districts in ways to develop and implement their K-6 Chemical Abuse Prevention Curriculum in the classroom.

Insight to the Oldest Child From an Alcoholic Family

By Cardwell C. Nuckols

Most adults view a child's world from their own frame of reference and find it difficult to imagine any life but their own as being stressful. Adult rememberance of childhood is often nostalgic, with fond recollections far outweighing the negative memories. The child's pain and stress seem insignificant in relation to their own. This model becomes exaggerated within the matrix of the chemically dependent family. How often are chemically dependent parents able to put themselves inside and feel the pain of their offspring?

As the chemically dependent family progresses along the continuum of illness, moments of pride and joy fade. However, there is one family member who can furnish a sense of worth and dignity when the usual means of family accomplishment no longer exist. Sharon Wegscheider uses the term "hero" to describe a role often taken by the oldest child in the chemically dependent family. The "hero" bears the impossible burden of the illusion that he/she can pull the family together. When consistency and structure are absent, this child often provides a sense of order for both parents and the other siblings.

Due to an overly responsible personality, the "hero" can, in certain ways, become a family enabler. At times, this responsible

19

child can work in concert with the spouse to postpone motivational crises. Motivational crises are events that confront the chemically dependent person with the reality that a pattern of progressive problems exists. These crises also reveal to the chemically dependent person the fact that they are not able to control or solve their problems. This type of crisis is often triggered when family members recognize the destructive nature of their enabling. Unfortunately, the chemically dependent family, working in concert, can postpone such a crisis.

Our "hero" also provides "excess" time for both parents by assuming aspects of the parenting role. The chemically dependent person has more time to drink or take drugs, while the spouse has more time to react to the dependent person. The "hero" might take care of the siblings by making sure their lunches are packed and that they are off to school on time. He/she may assume house cleaning and laundry responsibilities while the spouse devotes more and more energy to aiding in the family chemical dependency cover-up. The spouse now has more freedom to make excuses, cover up, and emotionally and intellectually support the defense systems of the chemically dependent person.

Due to birth order, the oldest child lives a favored existence for a time as an "only child." He/she is given center stage until another child is born, thereby removing this favored status. Though oldest children are skillful at gaining attention, in the chemically dependent family they find that mother and dad are too busy, too harrassed, or too unconcerned to tolerate demands. The outcome of this family struggle is that the oldest child trains him/herself for emotional isolation. The responsible child learns to rely exclusively on his/her own resources. They learn that the best way to accomplish a task is to do it themselves. They become extremely independent and appear able to stand alone. The "hero" becomes rigid, controlling, and adept at organizing. A great price is extracted and the oldest child often experiences extreme fear of being out of control—especially with regard to feelings.

Since our "hero" is obliged to pull the family together, he/she is operating under continual stress. He/she not only suffers under the pressure of this task, but unconsciously reminds him/herself of its existence and nearness. Any relaxation of deliberateness or purposeful activity is viewed as improper, unsafe, or worse. The oldest child feels guilty about taking time out to relax and enjoy childhood. Although the first child produces in quality and quantity, in their hearts there is a sense of uncertainty and emptiness. The family continues to deteriorate from the ravages of a progressive chemical dependency process.

The "hero" internalizes an obligation to correct the family imbalance. Compulsive drives to achieve impossible goals lead this first-born toward overachievement. Parents often take great pride in this adult-like youngster. Heroes are capable organizers and learn to manipulate to achieve balance and control. The abilities to structure and influence others, while being goal-oriented, provide the child with leadership qualities. These children may become enormously productive in socially-recognized ways. The activity—one could just as well say the life—of these people is characterized by a more-or-less continuous experience of tense deliberateness, a sense of effort, and of trying. Everything seems deliberate for them, nothing is effortless. It is not hard to imagine these children growing up to exhibit what is often referred to as the type "A" personality—those at highest risk for coronary disease.

Our "hero" suffers from two types of overload. The first is referred to as responsibility overload, and the second may be termed emotional overload. In terms of responsibility, it is not that our "hero" has to do physical labor, for children in the past did much more manual labor than children are expected to do today. There is a big difference, however. These children, especially our "heroes," are in a constant state of stress, secondary to the responsibility to hold the family together. While the family ship is constantly springing leaks, the "hero" attempts to bear the burden and slap on band-aids. There is tremendous emotional turmoil that is internalized within the chemically dependent family. Our "hero" is overloaded with fears and anxieties for which he may have no outlet. For example, if the child hears the family quarrelling, he has nowhere to turn to deal with the emotions surrounding the situation. As if there is a family "no-talk rule," family members are unable to talk to each other about the problems they experience, and it is especially "taboo" to talk to others outside of the immediate family.

While growing up, the family "hero" lives within an ongoing conflict between the child's needs and the demands of a rigid conscience. The child may attempt to ward off his or her unacceptable impulses and hence control anxiety by thoughts (obsessions), impulses to act (compulsions), or mixtures of both.

21

Often the obsessive thought or compulsion serve not only to help control and to prevent awareness of unacceptable impulses but, as a kind of double insurance, to emphasize the opposite of the unacceptable impulse. For example, when the "hero" sees his alcoholic father being abusive toward mother, he can react by giving himself a message such as, "The family must be OK because yesterday I brought home a report card with all A's. Only a good family could have had such a brilliant child." In actuality, there co-exists a polar opposite, but unacceptable, response of, "I hate you Daddy when you are mean to Mom." The former response protects our "hero."

There are secondary rewards to the "hero." His/her scholastic and athletic achievements bring praise and popularity. Quality and quantity of work bring opportunities to leave the physical confines of the family. Typically, the oldest child in the chemically dependent family leaves home for school or work. They seem not to return as a full-time member of the family, but continue to carry the unconscious message of their childhood.

Never having been provided with the proper parenting model that would allow the first born to achieve positive self-esteem, the "hero" is void of self-concept producing strategies. Although achievement-oriented, the direction of the achievement is not to satisfy personal needs, but to make up for perceived inadequacies and defects. These motivations stem from the "failure" to be able to correct the dysfunction of the family; feelings of guilt fuel and foster this inadequacy.

It is easy to understand why business and scholastic ventures are a primary avenue of overachievement for the oldest child from the chemically dependent family. Never having learned appropriate interpersonal strategies, and growing up in an unhealthy system, the "hero" will tend to avoid areas such as close intimacy and parenting where achievement seems difficult. Without proper strategies, the rearing of children and development of positive self-images take a back seat to the gratification achieved from business and academic worlds. Self-worth is predicated upon quality and quantity of achievement.

Understanding that the "hero's" beliefs about self-worth are unrealistic, it is easy to see how a vicious and rigid over-achieving spiral can evolve. Unconscious mechanisms to undermine achievement are often in place and represent a self-defeating flaw.

The first-born goes through life thinking that no matter how good he/she is, they must do better to afford themselves the luxury of self-satisfaction. The problem is complicated by an inflexibility of roles. The oldest child is locked into behavioral dynamics based on his perception of what needs to be done in order to survive.

Because "heroes" can produce competently in our achievement-oriented society, they are not looked upon as being in need of help. But they are ... and a sense of independence often interferes with their ability to ask for or accept this help.

Planning Community-Based Services for Children From Alcoholic Families

By Charles Deutsch

In recent years there has been a surge of interest in the offspring of alcoholics, both as children and as adults. The general public has been surprisingly receptive to the topic, in part because of greater awareness of alcoholism's prevalence and cost to society, and in part because of an increased belief (reflected more in rhetoric than in expenditures) in prevention.

Research on the population, most of it in the last decade, has confirmed the familial transmission of alcoholism, though the relative contribution of genetic and environmental factors remains unresolved. These findings have helped to stimulate new attempts to serve children of alcoholics. It must be conceded, however, that most of the other adverse health consequences which clinicians have associated with children of alcoholics have been inadequately studied. To evaluate these risks and our growing efforts to prevent them, we need to reach more children in more settings, and work more closely with researchers to produce non-threatening methods for measuring them.

The current interest in children of alcoholics, and the development of services for them, has come mainly from four different directions:

1. Alcoholism treatment programs, which are increasingly seeing the children of their patients as clients in their own right, not merely as potential facilitators or saboteurs of the alcoholic's recovery.

2. Al-Anon Family Groups, which were virtually alone in the field when Alateen was created in 1957. Although Alateen has grown consistently since then, Al-Anon acknowledges and is grappling with various obstacles to reaching more young people. In many areas, the increasing number of adult children of alcoholics attending Al-Anon has given rise to groups primarily composed of such members, and has contributed to a more general recognition of the need for alcoholism-specific therapies.

3. Through a variety of gradual processes, mental health professionals in more locales are becoming aware of alcoholism and its impact on children, and treating it as a central, rather than a symptomatic issue. This is an encouraging tendency and may have a ripple effect; but until instruction in the psychosocial effects of parental alcoholism becomes a standard part of clinical training for mental health workers of all kinds, it will be the rare therapist who pays enough attention to the impact and consequences of alcoholism.

4. Communities which combine quality alcohol education with safe and appealing resources have found that large numbers of children of alcoholics identify themselves and seek or accept sustained help. Unfortunately, very few communities meet both of those criteria.

It is important to understand where the impetus to serve children of alcoholics comes from, because the source is a crucial determinant of the service. The ways in which we conceptualize the children's needs and capacities; the goals and objectives around which we build interventions; and every structural and methodological detail that makes up our total program—all depend a great deal on the setting which brings us into contact with children of alcoholics.

My own work with children of alcoholics began in 1975 with the CASPAR Alcohol Education Program of Somerville, MA. CASPAR is one of the most widely replicated and nationally-respected primary prevention programs, and was probably the first to report the connection between systematic alcohol education and the ability to deliver a sustained intervention to a large, diverse, and previously unreachable population of children of alcoholics. In my subsequent writing, research, and consultation, it has become clear that approaching these children from a community-based primary prevention framework has brought me to principal assumptions, and an overall model, very different from the dominant programming approaches stemming from the treatment framework that characterizes the other three points of origin.

The first step in planning and developing programs for children of alcoholics is to form, however tentatively, a Big Picture: a conceptualization of the problems, goals, barriers, and strategies. The following assumptions, or tentative conclusions, summarize my Big Picture:

1. Most children of alcoholics are children whose parents are **not** in treatment.

2. Children of alcoholics can receive meaningful help whether or not their parents are in treatment.

3. The main problem in working with this population is reaching (that is, identifying and maintaining contact with) the children.

4. Reaching large numbers of the children most in need depends on a network of trained and motivated youth professionals, especially those who can mount group alcohol education activities.

5. Services must be carefully designed to maximize their accessibility, appeal, and security—in the absence of a sound structure, the content of services matters little.

6. For many children, a short-term educational/supportive treatment experience can lead to ongoing and more informal help, and stimulate important changes in feelings and behavior.

7. For most children of all ages, groups are the mode of choice; and peer-led groups should be seriously considered for adolescents.

Present space limitations prohibit elaboration on these seven points, but the basis for numbers (2) and (6) should be elucidated, however briefly. It is that most of the lasting damage which family alcoholism visits on children is a consequence, not of what parents actually do, but of how children construct images of self and the world, and how they behave according to those images, based on their interpretation of events in the home. Early intervention seeks to help children articulate their inaccurate and emotionally-devastating interpretations; to connect those interpretations, and their sources, with their behavior, often limited to certain rigid roles; and to reinforce and support a new understanding of this dynamic that is so central to their development. It is as if treatment replaces a fractured prism through which children see everything, and act accordingly, with glasses that let them see themselves and the world as it is, and like it much better. They see the same family experiences in a new light, and can change many of their responses. There is also good reason to believe that such children may be the most effective agents of change for their siblings and for their parents as well.

There are five stages in a systematic intervention process based on the seven assumptions just presented. Programs will certainly vary in how they conduct each stage, often based on such constraints as funding, level of agency cooperation, and community support. The trap, in planning and delivering services for children of alcoholics, is to overemphasize the actual treatment experience and pay too little attention, in both planning and executing the program, to the other four stages.

Stage 1: Pre-identification.

For reasons well known to those who work with them, most children of alcoholics will not simply appear at the door of a treatment resource, asking for help. A systematic program must have active strategies which will make it more likely that sizeable numbers of young people will identify themselves. Those people with whom the children and adolescents have frequent, natural, and safe contact, must be trained and motivated for the crucial but limited role of identification and referral. They may be teachers, guidance counselors, scout leaders, social workers, recreation workers; or they may be other young people trained and employed as peer leaders.

In general, the most effective gatekeepers are not counselors who work one-to-one, but those professionals and non-professionals who can conduct small group alcohol education. The reason is simple: the purpose of this stage is to make it more likely that kids will eventually be able to ask for help. Many children of alcoholics don't know the name of their problem, don't know it is their problem, don't know how to begin to talk about it. Through alcohol education, children who are not ready to name their problem aloud can still learn enough about it to make them more prepared to ask for help at a later opportunity, or when they simply feel more desperate or more hopeful. And as we will see, alcohol education itself provides them with numerous opportunities for sharing the responsibility of revealing the family secret they suffer so much for keeping. For this reason, all public education events, such as film screenings, staging of plays and puppet shows, and the like, contribute to a greater likelihood of identifying the children in need.

But sporadic public education events are not a substitute for a network of trained gatekeepers; and building such a network is a gradual and challenging business. Most human service professionals are overworked, underpaid, and underappreciated. Regardless of their discipline, they have usually had no training whatsoever in family alcoholism. Some are resistant because of their own drinking problems, or more commonly, because of unresolved experiences with alcoholism in their own loved ones. Most, whatever their backgrounds, have biases, fears, and reservations which trainers must respect, anticipate, and address.

Building a strong gatekeeper network and a solid pre-identification stage is a complex task, worthy of much more space. But if I should risk giving two simplified pieces of advice, I would urge refusing to undertake training programs of less than six hours; and using every available carrot and stick to get the gatekeepers you need in the same room with you for those six or more hours.

Stage 2: Identification.
Some children of alcoholics are identified by personnel situated to spot symptomatic behavior: probation officers, child guidance therapists, school and employment counselors. A much larger, more diverse, and probably more remedial group identify themselves to teachers, recreation workers, and clergy, particularly through group alcohol education activities. Trained peer leaders also greatly expand a program's identification capacities.

To identify these latter, less symptomatic children, programs must recognize, and equip gatekeepers to recognize and pick up on largely covert cues. Some children respond openly and directly at the first, long-awaited opportunity (most adult children of alcoholics can still recall how much they wished they had someone they could unburden themselves to). But the best many can do is leave a couple of trail markers; it may be an unconscious kind of test to see if the gatekeeper understands and cares enough to be trusted. Would-be helpers need to be prepared for these signs; and they need to understand them. They are not Stop signs; they are serious requests for help, simply made in the loudest voice the child can muster at the time.

Stage 3: Referral and Intake.

This stage involves the process by which the children, once identified, are lured to the first few contacts with the treatment resource. Programs can take various steps to encourage referrals; for example, they can schedule regular consultation appointments at the agencies which should be referring, instead of waiting for the phone to ring. But success in this stage has much less to do with actual referral and intake procedures, which are generally simple and straightforward, than with the structure of the resource itself.

The optimal resource is one that professionals know well, respect, and can rely on for accountability; one that is attractive and easy to sell to children; and one that minimizes the role the professional must play in transporting the child, providing information, and filling out forms. More important, from the children's perspective, before the treatment process can win them over, they must see enough in the program for themselves, and enough to protect them from parents and friends, to give it a try. The location and setting; time of day and duration; the people they meet and the nature of the first experiences; the built-in incentives and safeguards; and above all, the participation requirements: all these and other factors will have a decided effect on the ability to make and sustain contact with many children. Every effort must be made to make the resource as attractive and as accessible as possible.

Again, details are not possible in the present article. But a major issue which must at least be touched upon is the question of parental consent. If parental consent is required from the outset, a great many of the adolescents in greatest need will never surface at all. Although recent decisions in related cases have supported teenagers' rights to services (usually with regard to contraception or VD treatment where, unlike the family alcoholism situation, the parents are not the problem), the law is ambiguous, and in the end, almost irrelevant.

The question expands into ethical, political, and practical dimensions. If these children can indeed be helped without parental complicity, are they entitled to help, or must they be excluded? Can the program depend upon sufficient community support to offer adolescents an educational/supportive experience whether or not they inform their parents from the beginning? And can the program reach teenagers without logistic support from parents? Is the scenario of the enraged and litigious alcoholic family a real one? Are those children who participate covertly at greater risk than those who are barred from participation and kept in ignorance and shame? Obviously, these are questions to be considered in planning services if one assumes it is possible to reach out and help children of untreated parents.

Stage 4: The Group Experience.
The principal treatment mode is the small, closed, time-limited, structured group. The age range should rarely be more than two years. Two leaders are desirable, preferably one male and one female; and I recommend peer leaders, with no adult present, for adolescent groups. Leaders work from detailed lesson plans, with activities designed to promote maximum participation and to realize specific cognitive and affective objectives. Aside from being a place where consistency reigns, expectations are clear, and ventilation encouraged, the group must be a home for laughter and fun. The major treatment objectives are:

• Helping children learn a new way of understanding family alcoholism.
• Helping children evaluate, practice, and reinforce constructive coping options.
• Helping children feel better about themselves.
• Helping members clarify attitudes about drinking.
• Increasing children's receptivity to future help, including openness to friendship.

Stage 5: Reinforcement and Follow-up.
The children's further needs and capabilities, assessed during the group, are referred to appropriate agencies. The program

encourages and facilitates participation in Alateen, and, of course, offers services to other family members whenever possible. Periodic reunions are staged to promote friendships made in the groups. And the gatekeeper network so useful in Stage 1 provides reinforcement, and catalyzes further intervention for those who need it.

Community Prevention: Creating Choices for Children From Alcoholic Families

By Claudia Black

Community prevention can mean many different things ... public school prevention curricula, preventive measures to combat drinking drivers, public awareness seminars, media blitzes, are just a few examples. The key to effective prevention, however, is when every part of the community is willing to accept responsibility for its share and commit to action.

A critical feature of any successful community prevention program is to intervene **now** with the highest risk population for ongoing chemical dependency, namely the **child**—young, adolescent, or adult—who has been raised in an alcoholic home. Until communities offer direct services to this population, they have not made a serious commitment to prevention.

Unfortunately, many communities have been unwilling to develop direct services for our highest risk group. It is critical, therefore, that individuals and agencies within the community begin to explore the barriers—which are often attitudinal—that prevent the development of much needed services.

At its simplest level, prevention in the area of children of alcoholics means developing a process in which children of alcoholics are afforded the opportunity to make choices about how

33

they will live their lives. Children of alcoholics, largely due to the lack of services, are rarely given any choices. Consequently, they often become: rigid and inflexible; controlling; unable to play or relax; overly concerned with being in control, with an immobilizing fear of losing that control; powerless, helpless, without options, without choices; depressed; unable to identify needs; unable to talk honestly on an intimate level, with a tendency to discount and minimize feelings; highly tolerant of inappropriate behavior; fearful of feelings; unable to identify and express feelings, i.e., sadness, anger, guilt, embarrassment; overly fearful of authority figures; isolated; extremely critical of themselves.

Ultimately, many become alcoholic themselves, and/or stay in an alcoholic family system via marriage. This situation is inevitable unless persons and agencies within communities systematically organize. It is crucial that services be developed and implemented to:

(1) Educate children about alcoholism and the family. Clarify for the children what is actually occurring in their lives. Bring truth and understanding to their lives to eradicate the confusion of living with the dishonesty.

(2) Validate the child's experiences by offering acknowledgment of truth. In this way children are not so apt to deny, mimimize and rationalize the denial system which parallels that of the alcoholic and often the co-alcoholic parent. This "long-lived lie" will only work to aid in the development of their (the child's) own chemical dependency, if left unchanged. Validation gives them the feedback which allows them to see how their perceptions are accurate.

(3) Help problem solve situations in which children are left to problem-solve themselves with the intellectual, emotional and physical resources of just that—a child. By learning to problem solve with others who are able to be more objective, this child learns to be less controlling, dogmatic and rigid. In addition to discovering that there are good people on whom they can rely, they also begin to see themselves as more powerful and resourceful. In reducing their perceived powerlessness through effective problem solving, we help them see choices and options. While we will not necessarily be able to help stop the drinking, or change the co-alcoholic behavior, there are many areas in which these children can begin to exercise choice.

(4) Provide resources, give permission, and teach these children to play and relax.While at home they will most likely have to continue to be adult-like, extremely responsible for themselves and for others. We want them to know that outside of that home it is okay for them to be nine, or fifteen. They do not have to be adults! We want to normalize relaxation and spontaneity, in contrast to the tension and "rehearsal" which becomes normalized in the home. We do this by giving permission for playing and relaxing. When we cannot influence this directly, then we will influence it by referring them to play-oriented activities where they are available.

(5) Teach them to ask questions, rather than be so "all accepting." (This posture develops as the result of their perceived helplessness and inappropriate sense of limit setting, e.g., lack of clarity about their own limits of acceptable and non-acceptable behavior.)

(6) Teach them that they are **not** responsible for things over which they have no control.

(7) Reassure these children that talking honestly about themselves is not a betrayal of their parents.

(8) Teach and support them in their rights to stand up for themselves and/or ask for such protection from others.

(9) Reassure and reinforce their "loveability," that they have many fine qualities of unique worth.

(10) Help them find ways to express their anger, guilt, sadness, fear, disappointments and embarrassments, so that they are not self-destructive or damaging to others. As a child learns more options for letting their feelings out, and trusting the validity of those feelings, the fear of their own emotions is reduced.

Children are isolated emotionally, and many times socially and physically in alcoholic families. We need to assist them in reaching out to us ... to do that we must first reach out to them. People frequently become overly concerned about how to identify such children, and spend the lesser amount of their time developing resources to provide services. Communities already have access to these children of all ages, from infancy to the elderly. They are in our schools, churches, social service agencies, family service agencies, youth and recreational programs, juvenile justice facilities, within our own neighborhood, and within our own families.

The community has an important responsibility to communicate its availability to persons from alcoholic families. Through non-judgmental education, the manner in which services are offered, asking the appropriate questions, listening and responding to the answers, we will find that children of all ages are there to receive our efforts.

In conclusion, I am reminded of a 58-year-old adult child of an alcoholic who once said to me, "I spent my whole life making sure I didn't end up like my dad. Now, the only difference between my dad and me is that he died from his alcoholism ... maybe I don't have to die from mine." At 58, this man did not necessarily have a choice as to whether he became alcoholic ... that issue was moot. The question of his own mortality did not yet have a definitive answer, even in his own mind. But, what is important is that because this man was seeking help for his drinking, he had the beginning of a new choice which his father did not have.

And yet, this man should not have had to wait until he was 58 to learn that he has a choice. Maybe, if someone had intervened when he was 30 ... or 15 ... he might even have had an option about whether or not he became alcoholic.

Through direct services **to** and **for** the young, adolescent, and adult children from alcoholic families, we are offering them an important choice about how they will continue to live the rest of their lives ... that's prevention!

Conflict and Crisis Typify Life for Children From Alcoholic Families

By Rebecca Black

Reprinted from **The U.S. Journal.**

The emotional climate in a family with an alcoholic parent tends to be characterized by conflict and crisis, and family members are often angry and upset. Many of the estimated 10 million alcoholics in the U.S. are struggling to be adequate parents, while fighting the effects of a devastating illness.

In extensive research and clinical work done at Comprehensive Mental Health Services, Inc., of Boston, Massachusetts, one study cited that serious neglect of a child was determined to have occurred in 42% of the families with an alcoholic parent.

In 69% of the cases studied, abuse or neglect occurred alone, suggesting that they my be somewhat separate phenomena.

Studies of the general population indicate that from 3-4% of American parents abuse a child each year. This figure rises to 14% if hitting with an object, regardless of injury, is included.

Addicted parents who are abused themselves during childhood are more likely to have an abused child than non-abused addicted parents.

While it would be convenient to conclude that addiction to

alcohol causes abuse of children, this is far from clear. Addiction may be a cause of abuse or a consequence of abuse, or perhaps both. There may be an interaction between addiction and abuse resulting in the occurrence of both child abuse and addiction in the next generation.

It is possible that child abuse and addiction are not directly related, but are actually associated with other factors, such as poverty.

The incidence of child abuse and neglect in families with alcoholic parents appears to be three or more times higher than the incidence in the general population.

Addiction both directly and indirectly interferes with the time, energy, and emotional balance necessary for adequate care of the children of these parents.

Alcoholic parents, however, find these areas difficult to discuss, and tend to deny that any significant injury might be occurring to their children. They find it difficult to ask for help with their families, wanting to handle the problem alone.

Studies reveal that the family with an alcoholic parent is one in which overt conflict with the alcoholic occurs during periods of drinking; angry feelings are often acted out or displaced from the true target—the alcoholic; the source of the conflict—the drinking—is rarely discussed; the alcoholic attempts to recruit allies within the family unit in order to continue drinking, while shifting responsibility for the drinking onto other family members; the family is then divided against itself.

Alcoholic parents are spending so much time and effort to survive and get through daily crises that there is little time for the ordinary concerns of helping a child to develop.

Parents are not there to talk to, and they miss important events in the children's lives. Attention is also highly inconsistent. There are periods of little or no attention, when children are allowed to do as they please, and then there are periods of strict supervision and severe discipline. This inconsistency appears to be one of the most destructive aspects of these family interactions.

Children in these homes are always off balance, never knowing how the parent will behave and what will be expected. In very small children, there is serious interference with intellectual and emotional functioning, relating to this inconsistency.

The Family Law
In Alcoholic Homes—
Don't Talk

By Claudia Black

*The Family Law: **Don't Talk About The Real Issues.**
The real issues are: Mom is drinking again. Dad didn't come
home last night. Dad was drunk at the ballgame. I had to
walk home from school because Mom had passed out at home
and forgot to come and get me.*

*Some say it is a rule; I believe, for most alcoholic families,
it has become law. As one 9-year-old daughter of an alcoholic
said, "When you have a rule in your house for so long, not to
talk about dad's drinking, it's r-e-a-l-l-y hard to talk now
(even when he is sober)."*

In the earlier stages of alcoholism, when someone's drinking
seems to become more noticeable, family members usually
attempt to rationalize the behavior. They begin to invent excuses:
"Well, your dad has been working hard these past few months,"
or, "Your mom has been lonely since her best friend moved
away." As the drinking increases, the drinking and the irrational
rationalizations become a "normal" way of life.

Family members focus on the problems drinking causes, but
have difficulty associating drinking with those problems. An
excuse offered to a child I had been working with, for her dad's
irrational (alcoholic) behavior, was that he had a brain tumor and

was going to die. The mother told the children their father wanted them to hate him before he died, so it would be easier for them to accept his death when it happened. This now-adult person explains, "It didn't feel right, but who was I to question my mom? She had enough problems as it was." As a child, this woman believed her father was going crazy. She felt, "his going crazy seemed more likely than his going to die from a tumor." She now understands her father acted crazy, but his erratic behavior was due to his drinking and subsequent denial of his problem. His increasingly controlling and tyrannical moods, his inconsistent behavior related to his blackouts, as well as his open hallucinations added to his appearance of craziness.

It's easier to rationalize reasons, other than alcoholism, for crazy behavior. If the drinking takes place outside of the home, and dad doesn't act falling-down drunk when he comes home, or if they don't see him when he comes home, the children may more readily accept what the other parent tells them—drinking is not the problem.

If children do not understand alcoholism, it is difficult for them to identify their parent as an alcoholic. Children are like adults, in that they too will believe all alcoholics are old men on Skid Row, without jobs or families. One adult person said, "My dad loved me, and I knew that." No one ever explained to her that alcoholic people are also capable of loving others. She believed because her father loved her, he could not be alcoholic. She heard about alcoholism only once at church, where a recovering alcoholic told his story. But, what she heard was that particular alcoholic's perception of his own drinking. She could not relate this same type of alcoholism to her father's drinking. Her father certainly didn't sound, look, or act like this man who had been her only other contact with an alcoholic. Such fragmented information is typical of children's lack of knowledge concerning the disease of alcoholism.

Another way which helps family members rationalize the alcoholic's behavior is for them not to discuss or, in any manner, talk about what's really happening at home. Thirteen-year-old Steve said, "I thought I was going crazy. I thought I was the only one in my house who knew dad was an alcoholic. I didn't know anyone else knew." I asked him why he believed this to be true. He answered, "because no one else ever said anything." Steve described an incident which occurred when he and his father were at home alone. His father, in a semi-conscious state from drunkenness, was on the floor, had thrown-up, hit his head on the coffee table, and was bleeding. Steve's mother and sisters had returned home within moments after his dad hit his head. They just picked dad up and carried him off to the bedroom. No one spoke to anyone else. Steve said again he thought, "Maybe this is all in my head." I asked the two older sisters and Steve's mother why they had not talked about this incident with Steve. They responded, "because he hadn't said anything, and we hoped he hadn't noticed." I believe helplessness, despair and hopelessness cause family members to believe—**If you just ignore it, maybe it will not hurt; if you just ignore it, it may just go away.**

Many adult children have told me they were instructed not to talk about things which would upset mom or dad; or they simply learned by themselves that things went a lot easier when they did nothing to "rock the boat." One young man said, "Dinner was pretty quiet. Anything we said rocked the boat. And then, if we were too quiet, **that** rocked the boat!" These children not only don't talk about boat-rocking issues, but they don't talk about, or share their fears, worries or hurts with anyone.

Children will share the same bedroom with a sibling for years, both hearing the arguing taking place between mom and dad. Or, they hear mom crying night after night. But they only hear, they never speak to one another about it, although they may each cry— silently and alone. In one family, the six children were between the ages of 12 and 21 when dad sought treatment from alcoholism. Three to four months prior to seeking help, the father would return home late at night, after having been drinking for several hours. Not having seen his children all day, he'd make his nightly rounds, passing from one room to another, until he'd seen each of his children. He would scream, shout and harrass each child until moving on to the next room. All of the children were awake as he went from room to room, but they never spoke to each other about these nightly episodes. The family simply acted as though nothing out of the ordinary was happening.

In another family, young Billy told me how he was taking the air out of the car tires so dad wouldn't drive when he was drinking. His youngest sister, Ann, was putting water in dad's vodka bottle; his oldest sister, Lisa, was putting apple cider in dad's whiskey.

Each was unaware of the other's actions concerning dad's drinking because they were unable to talk about the **real** issue—their father's alcoholism.

Well-adjusted children who experience daily childhood problems would, most likely, talk about these problems with other family members. Because of the **denial** of the **alcoholism** in an alcoholic family, seldom are any of the children's problems recognized, and the family problem—alcoholism—is never discussed. These children (accurately, or inaccurately), do not perceive others, inside or outside of the family, to be available to them for help. Many adult children of alcoholics have questioned where their aunts and uncles were when they needed them. Nora told me if she had told anybody what her home life was like, she couldn't possibly have been believed. "They wouldn't believe me, because if it was so bad, I couldn't be looking so good. They never saw my mother getting drunk every day, they never saw her raving like a maniac, passed out upstairs. They never saw her bottles all over the house. They just never saw."

While many children fear not being believed, they may also experience guilt talking about the problems of their parents. They feel a sense of betrayal in talking about such delicate problems. Children find the family situation so complex and confusing, they feel inadequate in attempting to verbalize the problems—they just don't know how to tell others. Children feel very loyal to their parents, and invariably, these children end up defending their parents, rationalizing that it isn't really all that bad, and continuing in what has now become a denial process.

It is most despairing to be a child in an alcoholic family, to feel totally alone, and to believe talking will not help.

As Melody said, *"Sometimes I pretend my mom is not drinking when she really is. I never even talk about it."*

—Melody—Age 9

Understanding and Helping Children of Alcoholics

By Charles Deutsch

"With Martha, the problem occurred in another class, and that teacher said, 'Something is bothering you, and you've got to talk to someone—anyone you feel you can talk to.' She chose me, and came down and sat in my office for maybe an hour-and-a-half, and did not open her mouth except to cry. I said, 'Martha, you can stay here all day if you want. I'll make you a cup of tea and you can sit here, and when you're ready to tell me whatever it is you want to tell me, then you can just spit it out.' I had an idea what it was, but I didn't want to be the one to say anything, because I think that was her most important step, when she heard herself say, 'My mother is an alcoholic.' It took her an hour-and-a-half just to say the words, but once she got it out, everything was easy."

That was the day Martha began to get her life in order. At fourteen, she began to understand for the first time what was happening in her home and how it was making her feel and behave.

It was also the day she parted company with most of the roughly 15 million school-aged, American children who live with parental alcoholism. The great majority never achieve such understanding. Even as adults, most never understand enough about growing up in an alcoholic home to overcome its lasting effects on their emotions and behavior. However they try, millions of adults cannot come to grips with their present problems until they make sense of the parental alcoholism that was **THE** central reality of their formative years.

The growing awareness that alcoholism is a major public health problem, a chronic disease and not a moral failing or a criminal offense, has contributed to marked improvement in its treatment. By all accounts, more alcoholics are getting help each year, and the average age at which they reach treatment has dropped. There is also more help available for spouses of alcoholics, much of it provided by Al-Anon Family Groups. Al-Anon, a self-help organization, has four characteristics which are hard to beat: it's free, lifelong, everywhere, and extraordinarily effective for many people.

But children of alcoholics remain almost as neglected a population today as they were ten or twenty years ago. Alateen, a self-help organization sponsored by Al-Anon for adolescents who are worried about the drinking of someone they love, can be enormously beneficial to those who attend regularly. In addition, an increasing number of alcoholism treatment programs are offering services to family members, viewed not as potential accessories or saboteurs of the alcoholic's recovery, but as people with serious and treatable needs of their own.

However, the number of children actually reached through both approaches is relatively small, certainly not more than 5-10% of those living with parental alcoholism. And the great majority of these receive help only after either the alcoholic, or non-alcoholic parent has acknowledged the problem and sought assistance. Most children of alcoholics have no one, least of all their parents and relatives, who help them understand what is going on in the home, their own powerful and frightening emotions, or their own and their parents' inexplicable behavior.

How Parental Alcoholism Affects Children
"Once I had a problem and I was terrified to tell him. But he was okay about it. The next time I had the same feelings, he got up and started screaming, 'You never do anything right!' The unpredictability drove me crazy ... You don't understand what you did differently or how to connect again. It was really a total mystery about why one time and not another.

My mother was always complaining about his drinking, and she was busy theorizing about his behavior, but none of it made any sense to me. I used to wait for him in the seedy bars on Eighth Avenue, and I couldn't understand what could possibly attract him to this place and these people. It was a complete mystery to me."

It is crucial to understand how parental alcoholism damages children, both to evaluate the heightened risk for a variety of unhealthy patterns and illnesses associated with children of alcoholics, and also to understand why early intervention promises to be so effective.

Except for the minority of cases where there is actual physical (including sexual) abuse or neglect, the damage done to children of alcoholics comes not from what their parents actually do, but from **how the children interpret the events in the home**. Put most simply, the child's constant business is to figure out, by acting on the word, how s/he works and what the world is all about. S/he is constantly testing out, revising, and forming new notions about self and others, based not on what actually happens, but on how s/he interprets what happens. How s/he acts, inside and outside the home, is the direct result of the self-image and view of the world s/he constructs, mostly from family-based experiences.

Like other families, alcoholic families try to provide their children with the nurturance and safety they need. But the dynamics within the alcoholic family greatly impede that effort. In brief and simplified terms, children of alcoholics must contend with an environment characterized by inconsistency and fear; guilt and blame; anger and resentment; and pervasive secrecy and denial. The alcoholic, his drinking, the attempts to prevent or control the drinking, and the reactions to his drinking dominate the family. And this remains true, even after the alcoholic has left the home, died, or stopped drinking.

Because of the need to hide the drinking, the family is often isolated and cut off from other influences; this, in turn, makes the children even more dependent on whatever they can get from other family members. The rituals which should typically bond family members become instead their most painful battles. Far from developing a secure sense of its own balance and joint purpose, the family views its own existence as increasingly

45

precarious. And none of this is ever discussed! Children regularly report that they have never even discussed the drinking with their brothers and sisters The first thing they learn is that drinking is **the** most forbidden subject; or they are always hearing empty threats and broken promises. The end result is that words lose their intended meaning, and are used mainly to hurt and manipulate. Action (or inaction) and silence replace words as the principal methods of communication.

The roles themselves are not unique to children in alcoholic families. Growing up means trying on and adapting to different roles as situations change, and as the individual desires and capacities of the children change. The alcoholic family, however, is too insecure and fragile to permit flexibility. Since everyone feels responsible for causing the drinking, everyone feels responsible for dealing with its consequences and for trying to make the drinking stop. This effort is the key to family membership. It requires fidelity to narrow and rigid roles whose consistency lends the family some of the stability it otherwise lacks. In alcoholic families, these roles are not temporary or partial suits of clothing. Like spacesuits, they are crucial to survival. And, once inside them for a time, children (and the adults they become), have great difficulty operating outside of them. In addition, these roles are empty and unfulfilling because in each case their goal is unattainable: to stop the drinking and create a harmonious family.

For example, many families produce a **Hero**, a super-achiever incapable of giving less than his best in school and elsewhere, always striving to please. These children appear to be exemplary — having turned adversity into strength. Indeed, some children of alcoholics do just that. At the same time, many super-achievers grow into adults without a sense of their own entitlement, or the license to feel and show anger. They are usually perfectionistic, unable to relax, and convinced that however much they may be accomplishing, it is seldom, if ever, enough. Repeated career successes rarely bring satisfaction. Achievement was not, and is never an end, but a means to stop the drinking and win the love and nurturance that shouldn't have to be won.

Other children skip their childhoods. They cut off their emotions and become the **Manager's** of the family's affairs. As adults they remain exceptionally responsible, but aloof, rather joyless, always needing to be in control, and unaware of the source of their depression. They are the most likely to create situations in which they continue to play the role they know so well ... usually by marrying an alcoholic.

Still others retaliate, seeking both attention and revenge through adventures with the dangerous and destructive. The family **scapegoats** them for its problems—after all, they prefer believing that a child is "bad" to believing that of the adult upon which they all depend. Not surprisingly, the child forms a self-concept and an image of the world in accordance with this information. The result is the "Born to lose," or "You're certainly your father's son" outlook so characteristic of young people who go from one kind of failure or antisocial act to another.

"I knew that my father's drinking was affecting my life and making the whole family nervous and unhappy. But when I started drinking at about age 14, I never thought that my drinking had anything to do with my father's. I drank because I wanted to. I got drunk every time, just like him, but I never said to myself, 'Hey, you're drinking just like him.' "

Children At Risk

There are other roles and much more to read about them. The important point is that each is dysfunctional (though probably not equally so) because it is too rigid, exclusive, and unsatisfying. Each places the developing child in them at increased risk for a variety of adverse consequences. Some of these consequences have been thoroughly documented by researchers, while others are based on clinical observation.

There is conclusive evidence that children of alcoholics are at least twice as likely as other children to develop alcoholism themselves. Scapegoat children usually begin their abuse of alcohol and drugs early in life, with the accompanying educational, occupational, legal, physical, psychological, and interpersonal difficulties. Other children, including heroes, often begin as confirmed abstainers. However, recent research indicates that many develop problems with alcohol in midlife. The relative importance of genetic and environmental factors in the familial transmission of alcoholism is still unclear. In any case, most children of alcoholics have both factors working against them. The fascination and fear which alcohol evokes in them, the power it has in their memories and images, makes it an entirely different substance from the drink in the hands of someone whose parents drank responsibly or not at all. In fact, it's hard to see how we can cut down on future alcoholism unless we can systematically reach the children who have been groomed for it.

Children of alcoholics are often educationally impeded, comprising a disproportionate share of our annual school drop-out population, which goes on to be undertrained and chronically underemployed in adulthood. As one teenager put it:

> *"Lots of times I wanted to say, 'Hey, if you knew what it was like for me! I get it at home, and then I get it worse in school.' I wanted to say, 'How smart would you be if you had to lie awake in bed at night in case your mother got it into her head Could you concentrate in school if you were wondering what you were going to find when you got home?' "*

The most widespread consequences of parental alcoholism are psychological. Researchers are only beginning to study what clinicians have long noted: that children of alcoholics are more likely than others to be chronically depressed and suicidal; emotionally detached and socially isolated; and characterized by extremely low self-esteem. It is not difficult to see how life in an alcoholic family leads to these conditions, and how they, in turn, affect the kinds of interpersonal relationships many children of alcoholics form throughout their lives.

In addition, children of alcoholics often have an impaired sense of reality. When Ted was five, his mother used to tell him that she had stopped drinking, but he would find bottles hidden in the toilet tank. When he was ten, he was made to tell the neighbors that "Momma had the flu." There was a frequent discrepancy between what he wanted and needed to believe, and what he could believe. Children like Ted become dependent on, and well-practiced in denial. When they have threatening feelings or problems, they literally cannot recognize them.

The question of fetal alcohol syndrome aside, preliminary evidence indicates that children with alcoholic mothers are affected more severely than those with alcoholic fathers. Adolescent boys with alcoholic mothers are far and away the most difficult to reach. Since the mother is usually the primary caretaker and nurturer, her disability is more immediately and constantly felt by the child. She is also more often a single parent, as non-alcoholic husbands are more likely than non-alcoholic wives to leave their alcoholic spouses. Non-alcoholic husbands don't rely on their partner's paycheck and have not been inculcated since childhood with the responsibility for keeping the family together. However strong the stigma of alcoholism is for a male, it is much stronger for a female. It is widely believed that alcoholism among women, previously under-reported, is both more recognized today, and on the rise.

Helping

"I live with a feeling that I was shit all my life. If someone had said to me, 'You're not causing your mother's drinking, you're not responsible for her actions, you can't control it, you can't change it, and it doesn't make you a bad person,' I think that would have made a difference in my relationships as I grew up, and even now, in some of the issues I'm dealing with at my age."

It is generally assumed that it is the parent's drinking, and all of the behavior that goes with it, which places children of alcoholics in jeopardy. Those who accept this assumption conclude that the only substantial way to help the children is to help the parents recover. **This is the dominant and paralyzing myth.** Once we see the source of the damage as the child's interpretation of family events, and the self-image and defense patterns based on that interpretation, a very different conclusion emerges.

We can work to replace that interpretation, with its accompanying guilt, unworthiness, anger, and shame, with one that is both more accurate and more emotionally satisfying. These children see themselves and the world through a cracked and warped prism; their actions are consistent with their vision. We can help them discard the prism and understand what they see. And, we can be sure they will like what they see a whole lot more. The same family experiences can be understood in a totally different way. This understanding can lead to new, healthier, and more adaptive feelings and behaviors.

All of this can happen whether or not parents are in treatment—in fact, it can happen whether or not parents

know and approve. There are millions of children of alcoholics (most without parents in treatment), for whom serious adverse consequences can be prevented or diminished—if we can reach them and engage them in a relatively short-term, inexpensive intervention process. Furthermore, there is good reason to believe that such an intervention would benefit not only the kids who participate, but their siblings and parents as well.

At present, few communities have intervention resources that are both specifically designed for children of alcoholics **and** accessible to those whose parents are still caught up in denial and hopelessness. More resources will evolve **only** when we have learned to reach more children. Some of the difficulty in reaching children of alcoholics is inherent in the children themselves. Part of it lies within ourselves as would-be helpers, whether acting in a professional capacity or as concerned relatives, friends, or community members.

Children of alcoholics want to avoid discovery. They feel ashamed of their families and certain that no other family is like their own. They feel responsible for the drinking and the unhappiness. They have often been warned about revealing the family secret, either explicitly or by the silence that surrounds the drinking. Their own sense of loyalty is exaggerated by guilt, insecurity, and low self-esteem, resulting in their own need to deny the drinking they see.

Even with all of these powerful reasons to protect their secret and hide their pain, most children of alcoholics are desperate to talk about it, crying for a way to understand what is going on. The recurring crises in an alcoholic home, the love and bursts of hope, can help them overcome their fears and respond to the slightest encouragement. This is where our problem comes into play.

Most of us avoid the subject of alcoholism entirely, never creating an opening for the child, or setting up an atmosphere in which s/he can be honest. We still treat alcoholism as if it were a depravity not to be mentioned by decent folk. In our own silence we communicate to children that it is indeed something of which to be ashamed. We keep silent because we feel we don't know enough, assuming that one has to be an expert in order to help. We are afraid of invading privacy, overstepping boundaries, incurring wrath or causing tears (as if seeing tears is causing them!). Finally, we prefer to assume that if a child has a problem and wants to talk about it, s/he'll bring it up him/herself; and if s/he doesn't, it means s/he really doesn't want to talk about it.

Children of alcoholics need an invitation to talk about their feelings and problems. That invitation can be tendered by anyone with whom the child has some kind of trusting relationship, or some regular and natural contact, such as a relative, a teacher, a neighbor, a Scout Leader. The offer can begin with a simple expression of concern and a willingness to listen to whatever the child wants to say, **in complete confidence.** It may take several conversations, with one or the other of you doing most of the talking, before the subject of drinking can be raised. There are concrete ways would-be helpers can prepare themselves for these interactions. One of the most important is to remember that help is a gradual, incremental, and frequently imperceptible process.

Sometimes helping entails picking up on clues which the child leaves as a way of asking us to share the responsibility for discussing the forbidden topic. S/he may off-handedly mention the parent's drinking, allude to late-night fights, or be extremely negative about alcohol, equating all drinking with drunkenness. S/he may be bruised, malodorous, or reluctant to bring friends home. There are lots of signs that should lead us to consider the possibility that the undiagnosed disease called alcoholism is at work. It is crucial to remember that to begin to help the child, **we don't have to know much about alcoholism**—we can get the child to people who do. But unless we play our role, they will never get a chance to play theirs.

If we are ever to help more than a fraction of this most-remediable population we have to equip the community with resources to identify, reach, and treat large amounts of children with **and** without parents in treatment. This requires a collaborative effort by schools, youth agencies, mental health and alcoholism services, and community activists (including A.A. and Al-Anon members). A great deal of organizing, educating, and training is necessary to achieve this kind of collaboration. The program which could result will be much more accessible, comprehensive, and stable than one undertaken in isolation.

"You say, 'How can a teacher or guidance counselor make a difference when everything in the kid's world reinforces the

messages of shame and guilt?' But, I think it's like listening to a symphony. There may be an overwhelming amount of sound, but if the person sitting behind you is tapping his foot out of rhythm, you hear it. Even though it's one little voice, it's so dissonant with the message you've heard that it takes on importance. One voice speaking, when your whole world is shouting something different ... it can really make a difference. Especially if that voice is saying something that feels good to hear.''

Communities preparing to develop programs must carefully consider a range of design questions. Where and when will the program be held? What incentives and protections are offered to make participation easier at the outset? (Will parental permission be required?) Will individual, family, or group work be emphasized? What will the goals of treatment be? Who will run the treatment sessions? And, how do we expect to identify these kids in the first place?

Each state alcoholism agency has people who are either experts themselves, or who know where to reach one. **The main point is that we have to get started, and everyone can help.** Any kind of youth professional, any parent, and certainly any kid, can be the start of something big. By getting people talking to one another, learning, reading, thinking, calling attention to the need and enormous potential of a fairly simple and straight-forward intervention, making a few phone calls, bringing in a speaker, writing a letter ... we can begin. This is not fiction or hype. Many, if not most, good programs start as simply the gleam in someone's eye.

There are lots of kids, and lots of adults, too, whose lives can turn around if they a get a little help and support in understanding what their family experience has been. We can help them individually, and we can work to set up programs to help them systematically. What we cannot do is continue to ignore them. Too much is at stake for them, for ourselves, and for the combined futures of generations yet born.

School-Based Intervention Strategies for Children From Alcoholic Families

By Rokelle Lerner

The public school system in this country provides a perfect opportunity, both for prevention of chemical abuse problems, and intervention with high-risk children from alcoholic homes.

One of the most pressing societal and health problems today is the increased use of, and growing dependency upon drugs. Alcoholism, in particular, affects 35 million Americans, and is the third highest cause of death in the United States. One out of every 10 Americans is an alcoholic.

Drug abuse is a problem that cuts across socio-economic barriers and encompasses all age levels. It has been recognized for some years that children of alcoholic parents are subject to a high risk of developing alcoholism in their adult years. More recently, attention has been focused on the alarming high incidence of emotional and behavioral disorders among this group. Although the children of alcoholic parents may manifest disturbances throughout their development, they are most symptomatic in first grade and in early and late adolescence.

Children of alcoholic parents are three times more likely to become alcoholics than children of non-alcoholics. This is especially alarming in light of the estimates that children of

53

alcoholic parents in America exceed 28 million. Between one-fourth and one-half of all alcoholic persons have an alcoholic parent or close relative.

Preliminary research data confirms the observation of professionals in the field that these youngsters have a poor self-concept, are easily frustrated, often perform poorly in school, are more likely than their peers to suffer from adjustment problems in adolescence, and are more vulnerable to addiction.

In addition, there are indications that children who are exposed to parental alcoholism at an early age show more severe social and psychological adjustment problems in later life than children who first face this problem during adolescence. For these reasons, it is especially imperative to reach this younger age group. The needs of children of alcoholic parents are seldom considered by alcoholic treatment and prevention programs.

Alcohol intervention frequently fails to meet the needs of children who have been negatively affected by a parent's chemical dependency problem. The school system can provide children of alcoholics with the knowledge, skills and support to enable them to escape the heritage of dysfunction.

Dysfunctional families generate children whose behaviors surface in school. The behaviors that work for these children of alcoholics at home to provide distraction, divert anger and aid denial are generalized to the school situation. Educational professionals need to be trained to see the opportunity for intervention that is presented by this "acting-out" behavior. Unfortunately, there is still a wide-spread tendency to view this behavior as a need for disciplinary response and/or inappropriate labeling.

If a school can do little else, obtaining elementary curricula on chemical health education is an important first step. This is the first step to intervention with high risk children living with chemical abuse. In addition, the time to stop adolescent drug abuse is before it begins. All children can benefit from a well-structured drug abuse education program. Adolescence is a difficult time for everyone, particularly for the child who is handicapped by living with the effects of chemical abuse. Alcohol and other drugs are easy solutions to problems, and elementary schools can impact children while their values and attitudes are developing.

The need for effective drug education programs in the schools is imperative. Young people need facts and positive approaches to help them make sound decisions, should they be faced with group and individual pressure to misuse drugs. No single effort or auditorium type presentation can be considered a substitute for a carefully planned educational program.

Nationally, there is a lack of preventative drug education in the elementary schools. A study done by Dr. Mary Essef on Drug Education Curricula confirms that out of 280 schools surveyed, representing all parts of the country, 9.54% of 1,000 elementary school students were receiving drug education.

It is my contention that more emphasis must be placed on effective drug abuse education in the elementary schools. The school program for students must begin early. It is no longer appropriate to conceive of drug abuse education as a unit or course only at the secondary level. Concepts, attitudes and behaviors are developing during the elementary years, and the school cannot ignore this learning.

In the same survey by Dr. Essef, it was also noted that the type of drug education indicated by the majority of respondents was factual information orientation (90%). My experience in working with children shows that this is only the first step in drug abuse prevention. In order to educate our children, we must view the question of drug abuse, not just in pharmacological and legal aspects, but also in its psycho-social ramifications. Any understanding of drug use or abuse demands a presentation of factual information and a search for meaningful alternatives to the misuse of drugs. Ultimately, we must provide the students with an opportunity for informed, responsible decision-making. The common denominator that appears to limit the traditional methods of combating drug abuse involves the inability to get at the motives and needs behind drug abuse. They deal with symptoms and not the cause. An alternatives theory hypothesizes that people will stop taking drugs if they find something better, that they will be much less likely to start immoderate drug use if there are meaningful and satisfying alternatives. An approach which draws the connection between psychological/emotional factors and behavior, has proven to be a more effective preventative approach, than mere identification of different kinds of chemicals.

An important emphasis in implementing preventative drug abuse educational programs is the involvement of parents and community members. This is particularly imperative since chemical dependency is a disease that affects the whole family and, indeed, the entire community. The Inter-disciplinary Panel on Drug Abuse Information stated, "There must be cooperation and involvement of all other segments of the community in a joint effort with the school, if the mounting trend of drug abuse is to be reversed—melding of community effort is essential if the common objectives are to be met.'

Thus, preventative education of the elementary school level children must be implemented at the elementary school level if they are to be effective. There is evidence of drug involvement on the part of elementary school children, indicating a need for earlier education. At such a young age, children need assistance in decision-making skills to make responsible decisions about drug usage. They must be taught to distinguish between responsible drug use and irresponsible drug abuse, and that there are alternatives.

Since chemical dependency has reached epidemic proportions, our schools need to respond to this health hazard as they would any other epidemic. This response includes not only prevention efforts for all age levels, but also intervention programs for children of alcoholics.

There are approximately 28 million children in our schools, today, whose lives revolve around their parents' drinking. These children are more likely than other children to develop alcoholism in later years. These young people are in classrooms all over the country, and schools are faced with a challenge: to intervene with these children, or to allow this epidemic to continue.

Inadequate, Inconsistent ... Non-Existent Parenting: A Dilemma for Children From Alcoholic Families

By Thomas W. Perrin

In families with one or more alcoholic parents, children often suffer from inadequate or non-existing parenting. What is supposed to be too often isn't. The child must somehow adapt in order to survive an environment which is often hostile and rejecting. At the same time, the child tries to make some sense out of the incongruities in his or her life.

In addition to maladaptive defense mechanisms, children in alcoholic situations often develop more healthy, adaptive, mechanisms in order to deal with their situation. Common among these adaptive mechanisms is that of compensation, which refers to "the automatic and unconscious tendency to develop some physical, mental or emotional function to an unusual degree to conceal or make up for a deficit" (White and Gilliland, 1975).

Thus, the child in the alcoholic family, with one or more parents who are temporarily or chronically inadequate, seeks out substitutes or surrogates to fulfill those needs and wants which remain unsatisfied by the natural parents.

Alcoholic families are a focus of attention for several reasons. First, alcoholism in American culture is endemic. A recent (November, 1982) Gallup Poll (Television Broadcast), reports that one-third of American families have a member with a drinking problem, up from 18% in 1977 (Kenward & Rissover, 1980). Indeed, the incidence of alcoholism in America may be so great that, like the Mano of Liberia, we do not consider its symptoms to be problematic because so many of us have them (Alland, 1970). In a 1974 report to the National Institute on Alcohol Abuse and Alcoholism, the firm of Booz, Allen and Hamilton, Inc., estimated the number of children of alcoholics at 28 millon. A more recent estimate by Woodside (1982) puts the number of children of alcoholics under 20 years of age in New York State alone at 500,000. This number represents 9.4% of the New York population under 20 years of age.

Second, although the alcoholic family system is often chaotic and disorganized, alcoholic families behave in systematic and predictable ways (Jackson, 1954; Kellerman, 1969; Kaufman & Pattison, 1982). This effort further explores the dimensions of the alcoholic family system.

Third, despite a continuing social stigma surrounding alcoholism, alcoholic families are readily identifiable through treatment centers and self-help groups.

Fourth, persons who are now the grown-up children of alcoholic parents have a desire to tell their stories. One person interviewed had fantasized the interview years before having met anyone to whom she could tell her story. Years of isolation and ignorance caused by the stigma of alcoholism have left scars demanding to be healed by disclosure.

Fifth, and perhaps most significantly, the author is the child of two alcoholic parents. This writing, therefore, should be seen as part of a continuing personal search for the meaning and relevance of familian—and familiar—alcoholism. The author first became interested in surrogate relationships while attending a self-help group meeting of adult children of alcoholics. Since that time, the author, in his clinical practice, has routinely sought out data on his clients' surrogate parents while taking their histories.

A computer search of the literature revealed many items concerning surrogate parents for handicapped children, a result of Public Law 94-142's (Education for all Handicapped Children), requirement that surrogate parents be appointed to act for handicapped children who are without available biological parents. No titles relating to surrogate relationships in alcoholic families were found, however. Similarly, a review of the Rutgers Center of Alcohol Studies (Rutgers, 1982), current bibliography on children of alcoholics also revealed no such title. Four authors of recent books dealing with familial alcoholism (Black, 1981; Deutsch, 1982;

Wegscheider, 1982; and Woititz, 1983) do not mention the role of surrogate parents in alcoholic families.

Yet, the situation has not gone unnoticed. Russel (1982) asks questions about people other than biological parents who acted as parental figures in a survey of participants at a conference on children of alcoholics. A symposium sponsored by the National Institute on Alcohol Abuse and Alcoholism (1981) suggested that, given the special needs of children of alcoholics, the nature and content of treatment must be thought of in new ways. Among the suggestions made to therapists were the following:

- Offering the children a stable relationship;
- Allowing the child to borrow an ego for a while;
- Providing, in the person of a therapist, a co-parent or a substitute parent for a period of time.

A 1948 article by J. Evans entitled *"Johnny Rocco,"* provides a picture of a surrogate parent relationship. Johnny Rocco (fictional name), the son of an alcoholic bartender who was killed in a brawl when Johnny was five, was befriended by Jim O'Brien, then a counselor in an agency serving troubled boys. O'Brien took Rocco on camping trips and to museums. He bought, for example, the first birthday present Rocco ever received.

These activities were in sharp contrast to Rocco's other surrogate parent, his brother, Georgio, who, as the oldest child in the family, took over his father's role as wage earner and disciplinarian. Evans quotes Rocco as saying, "He (Georgio) used to give me Charlie-horses so's I couldn't move my arm. He broke my nose once. My head hit the door and I went out cold."

Konopka's (1976) account of adolescent girls indicates that grandparents are, next to parents, the family members who are often seen as the most beloved and in whom one can confide. Konopka's research indicates that the ideal adult for adolescent girls is the one who can listen and understand. This theme is accentuated by the Al-Anon Family Group's Guide for Sponsors of Alateen Groups. The guide asks sponsors (usually the only adult present), "Not to attempt to direct the proceedings or take part in the (group) discussion unless asked to do so by the members" (Al-Anon, 1974). It seems that the primary function of the adult sponsor is to listen actively to teenagers. The result, concludes the guide, is that the teenagers accept the sponsor and entrust him or her with many of their secrets and troubles.

Format

The purpose of this project was to explore, through taped

interviews, the boundaries and dimensions of the relationships which exist between the child and those adults whom she has chosen to replace her parents. Subjects for the interviews were volunteers among the friends and clients of the author. The author's insider viewpoint as the adult child of an alcoholic family was of great assistance in establishing trust between interviewer and interviewee.

No attempt was made to structure the interviews by means of a prewritten questionnaire. Similarly, no attempt was made to provide control groups for comparison. All of those interviewed were adult women. Consequently, differences in responses from adult men and minor children await further investigation.

The Experiences

The first choice for a surrogate parent in an alcoholic family was most often the first-born child. Sometimes the role was delegated to the oldest female, even if she was not first-born.

> ...*My brother, who was only fifteen years old by the time I was eleven. He ended up being the babysitter, the father, the mother, the brother, and took care of the three of us, and became an old man ahead of his time because of that. Super-responsible ... I sometimes wonder if his death in an automobile accident when he was 20 was a form of suicide brought on because of the responsibility.*

Another oldest child related that she "did everything that a parent's supposed to be." As a 26-year-old adult, this grown-up child of two alcoholic parents still retained some out-of-the-ordinary ideas of what a parent's role should be. In addition to "taking care of them," she stated that her role was "being an intermediary between them (her siblings) and my parents ... when my parents were angry at her (the youngest child), I always made sure she didn't get punished for it."

In many of the interviews, the oldest child is clearly an incompetent parent, often resulting to violence, as in the case of Johnny Rocco's oldest brother, Georgio. One older sister of a client in our practice resorted to burning her youngest sister's tongue with a hot poker in order to maintain discipline in the home. Understandably, these over-responsible children are often hated by their younger siblings—even when the relationship was not violent. Their role is symptomatic of the dysfunction and confusion in the family. The child voluntarily steps into the vacuum created by the alcoholic parent. The child feels guilty and believes, "If I don't do it, who will?" Decades later, the child grows up, marries an alcoholic or births one, and enables by doing for the alcoholic what he could not do for himself. This is the raw material of fusion in the family system.

We have successfully provided the mothers in these families with the injunction, "You don't have to do that," whenever they take on an inappropriate role in the family. We tell the parents that it is important for them to assert their role as parents. We ask them to impress upon their children, quietly, over and over again, like a broken record, "You don't have to do that. You don't have to be their mother or father. You don't have to be responsible for them." Not that, "You shouldn't," but that "You don't **have** to." In this way, the child comes to understand that he or she is under no obligation to be responsible for the younger children. They do not have to bear a burden that is inappropriate to their age and competence.

The oldest child, with no one to turn to in the nuclear family stressed by alcoholism, often looks to the extended family for an adult relationship. A grandparent, aunt or uncle provided the acceptance and support which the child needed.

(My aunt) told me about the goodness in me. And I had a very hard time believing that. And nobody else did.

My Aunt Ellen and my Aunt Rachel were two people that just unconditionally accepted me exactly as I was. And helped me out a lot just because of that. They just loved me. And they gave to me unconditionally.

Should the extended family fail to provide a surrogate parent, the child often looked to the parents of her friends.

Like my best friend in high school. Her mother was a surrogate mother. And before that, my best friend in junior high. Her mother was a surrogate mother.

The next choice often was a neighbor. A person who lived across the street, or next door, for example. The depth of the relationship became more superficial or more simple, the farther the child reached from home to find a surrogate.

And I used to sit on her porch every once in a while. We wouldn't talk or anything. I'd just sit, go on her porch, and she'd rock back and forth and I'd just sit there.

That's usually what I do. Take bits and pieces from different people, rather than the whole bulk from any one person.

This superficiality had several causes rooted in the reality of the situation.

Nobody moved in to a point where my parents became threatened enough as parents to do something about it ... and often my parents weren't aware of the extent of the relationship.

I was probably too needy at different times for people to be able to give more to me than they did give.

Paradoxically, the depth of the relationship between the surrogate and child was often more profound than its apparent superficiality.

During my teens, many adults acted as parent figures to me. Two of these traveled from the United States to England to attend my wedding there. My real parents stayed home. One of these surrogates was my grandmother. The other was a neighbor.

Depth of the relationships was often marked by how the children were affected by the death of their surrogate parents. In the case illustrated below, one might not normally assume that a relationship between a client and her father's girlfriend's mother would provoke an emotional response. Yet, the conversation came about because the client was visibly upset over the death of one whom, it turned out, was a surrogate parent. Viewed in this light, the emotional response is understandable and appropriate.

Nancy had gone to a friend's funeral on the weekend, and appeared quite sad during our session four days later. The funeral was for her father's girlfriend's mother, Mary, whom she had first met 11 years ago, and with whom she had maintained a close relationship over the years. Nancy saw Mary every two or three months. Nancy said that Mary was like a grandmother to her, but that they weren't that close. Yet, Nancy said, "Mary was nice and gentle. I could bring my boy friends to Mary. If my father didn't like them, Mary did."

Similarly, two other grown-up children of alcoholics related that they were deeply affected by the death of their surrogate parents.

I can only really remember one whose death got to me at all. And that was a man who just ... he was the father of a friend of mine, and he'd just hold me, you know, like anytime I'd see him he had a hug for me, and a smile for me, and he just thought I was great, you know, and that's all I needed, you know, that's all I needed from him.

And ... when he died, I think because of that, that really affected the rest of my life. Only one person who accepted me because of me, that was my only brother.

During the time she had cancer ... I saw her at least every other week, as often as I could possibly see her ... it was so much suffering during the year that I think I had mourned the year during the time she was dying. That I was accepting of her suffering ... I was accepting her death, but she's one of the few people that I cried at her funeral. I don't usually cry at funerals, and I felt a loss.

In listening to the adult children on these tapes, one notices over and over again themes of rejection and abandonment by natural parents, and unconditional love and acceptance by the surrogate parents. Implicit in these themes are multiple paradoxes: An alcoholic mother who was rejected by her own mother will reject her daughter—yet she will be the surrogate mother of her daughter's friends. Many of the subjects of these interviews chose surrogates themselves who were—or who later became—alcoholic themselves. For some parents, issues of guilt, counter-transference and control interfere with creating healthy relationships with their own children. The presence of alcohol or withdrawal from it prohibits the parent from working through these issues.

From the child's viewpoint, alcohol is rarely the issue. Perhaps children of alcoholics, like Konopka's (1976) adolescent girls, most "want loving parents who understand their children and were their friends, but also their protectors. They longed for harmony in the family." These qualities were absent in the families studied here.

The choice of surrogate parents in these interviews has been uniformly benign. One suspects, however, that when the choice of surrogate is benign, it is solely by chance. One can only speculate, at this juncture, what the effects are when the child chooses, or if chosen by, a gang, a physically, sexually, or emotionally abusive adult who initially or superficially accepts the child. The need for acceptance and love is so great that the child may endure the most severe indignities and exploitation in order to have these basic needs minimally satisfied.

Emotional Caretaking, Parental Roles and Self-Esteem: Three Personal Stories

By Jael Greenleaf

For the child growing up in a family with the alcoholism syndrome, the way to adulthood is frequently a minefield of inescapable dangers: violence, child neglect and physical abuse, incest, abandonment, brutal poverty, divorce, and the awful burden of trying to be parents to their own parents. The physical care-taking that falls to the children is harmful and confusing, but there is an insidious emotional caretaking that is more destructive because it is the least identifiable. Like a subclinical carcinoma, it eats away—not at the body, but at the child's sense of self. Physical caretaking is usually limited to the alcoholic parent. Emotional caretaking, on the other hand, is often demanded by the over-stressed co-alcoholic parent as well.

Whether they are alcoholic or co-alcoholic, parents whose self-esteem is poor will set a low ceiling on self-esteem in their families; if they are unsure of their ability to cope, they will be threatened by another's competence; if they feel inadequate, they will be envious of others' achievements; if they are confused, they will bestow confusion on those around them; and if their expectations of themselves are unrealistic, they will have unrealistic expectations of others. If they hate themselves, they will have little love to give. They cannot give to their children, or to each other, what they themselves do not have. The damage that they cause is in no way intentional. They do not know how to do better—they are doing their best already.

The harm that stems from children assuming responsibility for their parents' well-being is often very subtle. Each incident would do little harm in a child's life if it happened only once, or even two or three times, but like water wearing away stone, the erosion of the self is gradual, the result of years of repeated shame, embarrassment, humiliation and insult.

In the stories that follow, it must be understood that the incidents described were not one-time occurrences—they were the child's constant experiences. The corrosive attitude was in the atmosphere, like smog. We must also remember that children do not have either the structural or the emotional option to abandon their parents. Regardless of how they may feel later on when they, themselves, are adults, little children love their parents with unqualified, unquestioning love, and will do anything they can to protect them. Children do not yet have common sense, they have only uncommon love. (All names and identifying information have been changed to protect anonymity.)

ANNE
"When I was in grade school, my mother told me that she was going to be one of the four volunteers who came to the class to take the kids on field trips. She was pleased with the idea and it was clear to me that I was supposed to be pleased too. I wasn't pleased. I was frightened and angry—frightened that she would come to school drunk, that the kids would make fun of her, that she would be hurt by them, that she would get physically hurt falling down on the school's marble floors, that she'd slip away to a bar during a trip and forget to come back for us. Mostly, I was frightened that she was so fragile, so terribly fragile, that she didn't even see how inappropriate it would be for her to come to school at all. She was trying so hard to be a "good mother," to be competent at the only task that my father allowed her. I just couldn't tell her that I hated the idea. I couldn't let my feelings show because I knew, from past experience, that she would be hurt, cry, get drunk, be depressed and maudlin for weeks afterward, and that every time she was drunk she'd want to talk to me about her pain and sorrow that our relationship wasn't cozy.

When she and the other mothers came to school, I sat frozen in my seat, silent and rigid, watching out of the corner of my eye, ashamed and embarrassed by her pathetic pride; angry that she had invaded the one and only place where an adult took care of me, the one place that I could pay attention to other things and be free. The only safe place that I had to simply be myself became her arena and I, again, had to exist for her safety. It was horrifying—it felt like watching myself disappear. I was six years old.

Over the next twenty years of her life, I learned not to be interested in anything, because my drunken mother would stagger in, pathetically wanting attention. The only way that I could be left alone was to be depressed and withdrawn. I spent 35 years of my life in pain, rage, and despair, as I felt my sense of self evaporate into unquestioned obligation whenever I was around helpless, pathetic people. Seven years ago, I hit bottom emotionally. I was dying from the inside out and I knew it, knew it so vividly that I could not go on offering myself up as a sacrifice to the chronically desperate, donating me to the infinitely needy. Gradually, my knee jerk response faded and finally vanished. Now, I am willing to help those who need a hand, but I can walk away from professional victims, not with rage and fear, not with pity or numbness, but with profound sorrow for their distorted lives. "

The speaker is a 42-year-old executive woman.

JEFFREY

"The most prevalent feelings in my house were disgust and pity—very quiet disgust and pity. Me? I was confused, frightened and depressed. Not frightened by them, they were both non-violent, very repressed people. No, I was frightened for them. They seemed so helpless ... like tragic giants. When they died, my mother from alcoholism, my father from a variety of psychosomatic diseases, it was like Gotterdammerung—The Twilight of the Gods. They were finally at peace with their failure to survive. I don't miss them ... I never knew them. We were all characters in a sick and sickening drama. Even as a very young child, I knew that my life depended on being best supporting actor

to their tragic heroes. *Maybe that's why I went into the entertainment business, and why I'm still uncomfortable in the title role. My whole life, I've taken cues from someone else. How could I play Hamlet when I felt like poor Yorick?*

"*As I said, my family was fairly quiet, and in some ways that was the most confusing to me later on, when I would hear the alcoholic family described as loud, violent, and constantly fighting. No one in my family ever yelled and there was certainly no violence or physical abuse. It was a subtle, crazy-making ordeal. My father was athletic and expected me to be the same way, even though a childhood illness prevented me from being in rough and tumble activities. He settled for bowling and three times a week we would all set out on the awful trek to the local lanes. It was grim. He watched my mother with silent disgust and then shifted his attention to everything I did, constantly criticizing every move, forcing me to re-do impossible setups. I just spaced out and felt like an automaton—it was the only way I could escape his constant criticism—just go numb. I couldn't disobey him, or tell him to back off; he'd sulk for weeks and make snide remarks about anything I did. Or, he would go into my room and take things—my letters, my toys, anything that I cared about would just disappear.*

"*When I got interested in theater, he tolerated it at first—after all, I was only in the fourth grade. But as I began getting parts in community productions—the first when I was about eleven—the tension grew. He was so competitive with me and I had gone into an area in which he could not compete. He was left out of the spotlight, couldn't tell me how to do it right, couldn't control me or the play, couldn't be a big shot. He could, however, humiliate me. I was forbidden to have the professional photographs that were taken for promotion. No—the only photos allowed were the ones **he** took, even though he came to only one or two performances a year. His were always embarrassing. His favorite was of me in the seventh grade play, carrying a tray of glasses, tripping over a misplaced prop and falling off the stage. He carried the picture with him and whenever anyone would ask how my acting was coming, he would pull out the snapshot and say, 'Jeffrey wasn't satisfied with a* bit part, so this is how he got the lead.' I must have heard that line thousands of times before I was 18. Finally, I got hold of the picture and burned it. There were two conflicting messages—'If you aren't perfect, I won't love you ... If you try to be perfect, I'll compete with you and destroy you.'

"It's funny. There are six of us kids and we all have mixed feelings about our alcoholic mom, but we all love her. There are no mixed feelings about my co-alcoholic father; we all hate him."

The speaker is a 37-year-old actor.

SUSAN

"We were desperately poor. There were five of us crammed into a two-room apartment near the mill where my father worked. Even when he was not drunk, he would bait me all during dinner. He would ask me what I had done all day and if I began to tell him, he'd interrupt and ask in a sneering tone, 'What makes you think anybody wants to hear all that drivel?' If I said, 'Oh, nothing,' or 'Not much, he'd turn on my mother and ask her what kind of lazy slob she was raising.

"School, academic achievement, and intelligence were very dangerous subjects whenever he was around. I was a good student and I loved school. When report cards came out, I always got straight A's, and written comments from the teachers that I was bright and ahead of my classmates, etc. I always tried to get my mother to sign the card and return it to school before my father saw it. If he got hold of it, he would back me into a corner, shake his fist in my face, and yell, 'You think you're so smart. You think you're better than everybody. Well, let me tell you, you don't do the thinking around here. I do. If I had all the advantages you have, I'd be a millionnaire. You're not so hot, you're just a dumb brat. I've got more brains in my little finger than you do in your whole head.' And on and on, towering over me, shaking his fists, until he would quit in disgust and begin drinking. Then he'd cry and blubber about how hard he tried to get ahead. I felt ashamed and frightened. I didn't understand how, by being smart, I had hurt my father. I was more frightened by his crying jags than I was by

69

his rage. When he was raving, I knew what was happening and I knew that it would run its course. When he was sobbing and moaning, I was terrified that he would die, and at that time I still loved him. It didn't occur to me not to love him. He was my father.

"I learned to play dumb to protect them. But in the sixth grade, the school sent our IQ scores home. My IQ was considerably higher than his, and after ranting at me for two or three days, my father went on a sullen binge, refusing to speak to me for two months. He spoke to everyone else, but would only sneer at me, saying, 'Her highness (only he pronounced it hind-ass) is too good to talk to slobs like us.'

"My father had dropped out of school in seventh grade and when I entered the eighth grade I went into a panic. I was terrified that he would become depressed and angry and attack me. He didn't seem to notice, but I lived that whole year in terror. My fear waned during the summer, then went up at the end of August before school started. I kept waiting for the ax to fall. I didn't realize that he had simply written me off. I was a non-person.

"All through school I continued to play dumb when anyone was around. I thought that I was a freak and that if I publicly displayed intelligence, other people would be overwhelmed, angry and depressed. I felt that I somehow had the power to destroy other people simply by being intellectually competent. I considered myself a dangerous being who had to be controlled for other people's safety as well as my own. Although I've gained more perspective on it over the years, I still look for clues in other people to see how much mental power is okay before I get zapped. I vacillate between feeling incompetent, that is, I did it wrong, I failed, and being too much, that is, I did it too well, I misused it, someone will suffer."

The speaker is a 47-year-old psychologist.

Although the class backgrounds and styles of alcoholism are very different in these three brief biographies, the commonalities are many. We see parents who are frightened, insecure and self-hating. It is not that they could be good parents if they tried harder; they are simply raising their children as they were raised. Five out of the six parents were, themselves, raised with alcoholism, and they suffered the same abuses as their children. We see parents who do not know where they stop and their children begin, who are confused and confusing, who, out of their own anxiety and self-hatred, lash out brutally or subtly at the most available targets. We see children who live in fear that they will somehow harm or destroy their parents; who have no choice but to focus constantly on other people; who view other people's intrusions into their psyches as sad, but inevitable; who fear that if they demonstrate healthy self-satisfaction, that something nebulous and horrible will happen. As Jeffrey put it, "If I had it all—a good relationship, a good career, a nice car, good friends—I knew that 'they' would just 'beam me up,' but there wouldn't be a space ship to land on—just nothingness."

While the portraits in these biographies may seem unduly grim, they were chosen—not for their dramatic effect—but because they are typical. The only unusual aspect is that the speakers have sufficient healing behind them to remember and to articulate their experiences. The crazy-making confusion, the mixed messages, the lack of outside resources or points of reference, and the legitimate, near total dependency of chidren makes it difficult for them, even as adults, to recall what happened, let alone to understand how it affected them.

They are not used to understanding themselves, they are used to controlling themselves and understanding others. As Susan said, "I had no time to understand myself. I was busy understanding them. I was the watcher watching; always taking a reading on everyone around me. I nearly understood my life away."

For Anne, Jeffrey and Susan, life is much different today than it was when they were children. They have learned to care about and for themselves, as well as others. All children, whether young or adult, have this potential, and we dare not dismiss them simply because they cannot tell us where or how it hurts.

Children of Alcoholics— The Clinical Profile

By Claudia Black

The clinical profile of children from alcoholic homes has been largely based upon observation in the therapeutic setting, disclosure in adult children's support groups, and interpretation of children's artwork. CoA's are depicted as isolated, unable to identify and express feelings, unable to trust, be honest, or otherwise form solid, intimate relationships, and often misdiagnosed and misidentified by a wide range of professionals working with kids. However, as accurate a description as this may sound, research support which lends validity to this picture has been lacking.

A recent study completed by Claudia Black, comparing a sample of 400 adult children of alcoholics to a sample of controls not raised in alcoholic environments, provides some verification of the aforementioned clinical profile.

The primary indicator of a childhood environment permeated with alcoholism was "the inability to accurately identify what one needs," particularly as this relates to emotional needs. Seventy-four percent of the CoA's were unable to do this. Correlated strongly, and not surprisingly with this inability—the inability to "place themselves first" on their own priority lists (65%).

Intimacy was viewed by 72% of the CoA group as a major problematic area of adult life, compared to 40% of the controls. Black proposed honesty as the core element of this problem area. "It has to be," she stated. "If I cannot accurately identify my feelings, I cannot tell you what I need. If I cannot honestly tell you what I need, I cannot hope to build real intimacy, so I end up isolated."

That isolation and the subsequent withdrawal from social contact is a significant problem was demonstrated by the fact that 45% of the CoA group identified depression as a major problem. This compared to only 23% of the controls.

"The 'No Talk' rule permeates every aspect of these kids' lives," stated Black. "The alcoholic must deny his or her drinking, they can't be honest with themselves or anyone else. Because they have been told not to talk to anyone, most of these kids don't even use other people within the family to talk about the real problems.

Black surveyed her study participants as to whom they talked, whom did they use as a resource inside and outside the family? Fifty-three percent of the CoA group never once spoke to anyone about what was taking place at home. Forty-seven percent of this group did use the other parent at times, but only 8-9% with any regularity. Only 5-6% used a brother or a sister. Fifty-five percent of the CoA's never made use of siblings; had never discussed their parents' drinking!

Twenty-seven percent of the CoA group did indicate that they made use of their friends. However, this was in contrast to a 68% figure among the controls.

When queried about the use of "professional or other resource" people outside the home, the statistics are even less encouraging. Only 10% of the CoA's were willing to use teachers or school counselors; two times less likely than the controls. Clergy and doctors were utilized only 8% of the time, a figure reflecting one-third less likelihood of the controls.

"We, as kids, are taught that the clergy and medical people are the ones who can help the most, outside our own families, with problems," stated Black. "But when they can't use the people in their own family as a resource, what makes us think that as professionals, kids are going to be willing to talk to us? They are afraid, ashamed, embarrassed, and see themselves as betrayers of the 'family secret.'

"What we, as professionals, need to do is to help these kids understand that in fact, there is a sickness going on in their home ... it's not their fault, they're not responsible, they don't need to be ashamed, feel guilty, or feel that they've committed treason.

"Our responsibility is to each do our own part. Increased identification and awareness will result in more accurate diagnosis in the schools and clinical settings. Services can then be effectively designed to end this legacy of isolation, lack of intimacy, and angry, depressed adults ... not to mention reduce the risk of creating a subsequent generation of alcoholics."

Common Characteristics of Adult Children From Alcoholic Families

By Janet G. Woititz

The child grows into an adult. We all know what an adult is ... until we are asked to define the word. When we begin to **search** for the answers, we wonder. What is the definition of an adult? You have to define it for yourself. Maybe it's the point in your life when you are where the buck stops. Maybe that's when you become an adult ... the time when you are in charge of your life.

You have a lot of questions, many of which lead to new questions. Because your foundation has been ambiguous, you've always had a lot of questions. You may not even have known what all those questions were, but one thing was clear. You didn't have a lot of answers.

The list that follows is not the result of a scientific survey. It is a consensus of statements that adult children of alcoholics have made about themselves. They may not all be true for you, or they may only be true to some degree. It's a way to show you that some of the things that have caused you to wonder about your emotional health are carryovers from your childhood.

1. Adult children of alcoholics guess at what normal is.
The significance of this statement cannot be overestimated, as it

is their most profound characteristic. Adult children of alcoholics simply have no experience with what is normal.

After all, when you take a look at your history, how could you have any understanding of normalcy? Your home life varied from slightly mad to extremely bizarre.

Since this was the only home life you knew, what others would consider "slightly mad" or "extremely bizarre" were usual to you. If there was an occasional day that one could characterize as "normal," it certainly was not typical, and therefore could not have had much meaning.

Beyond your chaotic day-to-day life, part of what you did was to live in fantasy. You lived in a world that you created all your own, a world of what life would be like IF ... what your home would be like IF ... the way your parents would relate to each other IF ... the things that would be possible for you IF ... And you structured a whole life based on something that was probably impossible. The unrealistic fantasies about what life would be like if your parent got sober probably helped you survive, but added to your confusion.

It becomes very clear that you have no frame of reference for what it is like to be in a normal household. You also have no frame of reference for what is O.K. to say and to feel. In a more typical situation, one does not have to walk on eggs all the time. One doesn't have to question or repress one's feelings all the time. Because you did, you also became confused. Many things from the past contributed to your having to guess at what normal is.

2. Adult children of alcoholics have difficulty in following a project through from beginning to end.

The topic one evening in an adult children of alcoholics meeting was procrastination. When I asked the group members to talk about what it meant to them, the opening response was, "I'm the world's biggest procrastinator," or "somehow I just don't seem to be able to finish anything that I start."

These comments are fairly typical, and it's not too hard to understand why a difficulty exists. These people are not procrastinators in the usual sense.

The great job was always around the corner. The big deal was always about to be made. The work that needed to be done around the house would be done in no time ... the toy that will be built ... the go-cart ... the doll house ... and on and on.

"I'm going to do this, I'm going to do that." But this or that never really happened. Not only didn't it happen, but the alcoholic wanted credit for even having the idea, even for intending to do it. You grew up in this environment.

There were many wonderful ideas, but they were never acted on. If they were, so much time passed that you had forgotten about the original idea.

Who took the time to sit down with you when you had an idea for a project and said. "That's a good idea. How are you going to go about doing it? How long is it going to take? What are the steps involved?" Probably no one. When was it that one of your parents said, "Gee, that idea is terrific! You sure you can do it? Can you break it down into smaller pieces? Can you make it manageable?" Probably never.

This is not to suggest that **all** parents who do not live with alcohol teach their children how to solve problems. But it is to suggest that in a functional family, the child has this behavior and attitude to model. The child observes the process and the child may even ask questions along the way. The learning may be more indirect than direct, but it is present. Since your experience was so vastly different, it should be no surprise that you have a problem with following a project through from beginning to end. You haven't seen it happen and you don't know how to make it happen. Lack of knowledge isn't the same as procrastination.

3. Adult children of alcoholics lie when it would be just as easy to tell the truth.

Lying is basic to the family system affected by alcohol. It masquerades in part as overt denial of unpleasant realities, coverups, broken promises, and inconsistencies. It takes many forms and has many implications. Although it is somewhat different from the kind of lying usually talked about, it certainly is a departure from the truth.

The first and most basic lie is the family's denial of the problem.

So the pretense that everything at home is in order is a lie, and the family rarely discusses the truth openly, even with each other. Perhaps somewhere in one's private thoughts there is a recognition of the truth, but there is also the struggle to deny it.

The next lie, the cover-up, relates to the first. The non-alcoholic family member covers up for the alcoholic member. As a child, you saw your non-alcoholic parent covering up for your alcoholic parent. You heard him or her on the phone making excuses for your mother or father for not fulfilling an obligation, not being on time. That's part of the lie that you lived.

You also heard a lot of promises from your alcoholic parent. These, too, turned out to be lies.

Lying as the norm in your house became part of what you knew and what could be useful to you. At times it made life much more comfortable. If you lied about getting your work done, you could get away with being lazy for a while. If you lied about why you couldn't bring a friend home, or why you were late coming home, you could avert unpleasantness. It seemed to make life simpler for everyone.

Lying has become a habit. That's why the statement, "Adult children of alcoholics lie when it would be just as easy to tell the truth," is relevant. But if lying is what you have heard comes naturally, perhaps it is not as easy to tell the truth.

In this context, "it would be just as easy to tell the truth," means that you derive no real benefit from lying.

4. **Adult children of alcoholics judge themselves without mercy.**

When you were a child, there was no way that you were good enough. You were constantly criticized. You believed that your family would be better off without you, because you were the cause of the trouble. You may have been criticized for things that made no sense. "If you weren't such a rotten kid, I wouldn't have to drink." It makes no sense, but if you hear something often enough, for a long-enough period of time, you will end up believing it. As a result, you internalized these criticisms as negative self-feelings. They remain, even though no one is saying them to you anymore.

Since there is no way for you to meet the standards of perfection that you have internalized from childhood, you are always falling short of the mark you have set for yourself. As a child, whatever you did was not quite good enough. No matter how hard you tried, you should have tried harder. If you got an A, it should have been an A+. You were never good enough. A client told me that his mother was so demanding that when he was in basic training, he found the sergeants loose. So this became a part of you ... who you are, a part of the way you see yourself. The "shoulds" and "should nots" can become paralyzing after a while.

Your judgment of others is not nearly as harsh as your judgment of yourself, although it is hard for you to see other people's behavior in terms of a continuum either. Black and white, good or bad, are typically the way you look at things. Either side is an awesome responsibility. You know what it feels like to be bad, and how these feelings make you behave. And then, if you are good, there is always the risk that it won't last. So, either way, you set yourself up. Either way there is a great amount of pressure on you all of the time. How difficult and stressful life is. How hard it is to just sit back and relax and say, "It's O.K. to be me."

5. Adult children of alcoholics have difficulty having fun.
6. Adult children of alcoholics take themselves very seriously.

These two characteristics are very closely linked. If you're having trouble having fun, you're probably taking yourself very seriously, and if you don't take yourself all that seriously, chances are you can have fun.

Once again, in order to understand this problem, you need to look back at your childhood. How much fun was your childhood? You don't have to answer that. Children of alcoholics simply don't have much fun. One child of an alcoholic described it as "chronic trauma." You didn't hear your parents laughing and joking and fooling around. Life was a very serious, angry business. You didn't really learn to play with the other kids. You could join in some of the games, but were you really able to let yourself go and have fun? Even if you could have, it was discouraged. The tone around the house put a damper on your fun. Eventually, you just went along with everyone else. Having fun just wasn't fun. There was no place for it in your house. You gave it up. It just wasn't a workable idea. The spontaneous child within was squashed.

Having fun, being silly, being child-like, is to be foolish. It is no wonder that adult children of alcoholics have difficulty having fun. Life is too serious.

You also have trouble separating yourself from your work, so you take yourself very seriously at whatever job you have to do. You can't take the work seriously and not yourself. You are therefore a prime candidate for burnout.

One night a client turned to me with a very angry face and said, "You make me laugh at myself, but I want you to know I don't think it's funny!"

7. Adult children of alcoholics have difficulty with intimate relationships.

They want very much to have healthy, intimate relationships, but it is extraordinarily difficult for a number of reasons:

The first and most obvious is that they have no frame of reference for a healthy, intimate relationship because they have never seen one. The only model they have is their parents, which you and I know was not healthy.

They also carry with them the experience of "come close, go away," the inconsistency of a loving parent-child relationship. They feel loved one day and rejected the next. The fear of being abandoned is a terrible fear they grow up with. If the fear isn't overwhelming, it certainly gets in the way. Not knowing what it is like to have a consistent, day-to-day, healthy, intimate relationship with another person makes building one very painful and very complicated.

The fear of abandonment gets in the way of the developing of a relationship. The development of any healthy relationship requires a lot of give and take, and problem-solving. There is always some disagreement and anger which a couple resolve. A minor disagreement gets very big very quickly for adult children of alcoholics, because the issue of being abandoned takes precedence over the original issue.

These overwhelming fears of being abandoned or rejected prevent any ease in the process of developing a relationship.

Coupled with a sense of urgency, "This is the only time I have; if I don't do it now, it will never happen," tend to put pressure on the relationship. It makes it much more difficult to evolve slowly, to let two people get to know each other better, and to explore each other's feelings and attitudes in a variety of ways.

This sense of urgency makes the other person feel smothered, even though it is not the intent. I know a couple who have tremendous problems, because whenever they argue she panics and worries that he is now going to leave her. She needs constant reassurance in the middle of the argument that he's not going to leave her, and that he still loves her. When he is in conflict, which is difficult for him as well, he tends to want to withdraw and be by himself. Needless to say, this makes the issue at hand more difficult to resolve that if it were only the issue itself needing to be confronted.

The feelings of being insecure, of having difficulty in trusting, and questions about whether or not you're going to get hurt are not exclusive to adult children of alcoholics. These are problems most people have. Few people enter a relationship fully confident that things are going to work out the way they hope they will. They enter into a relationship hopeful, but with a variety of fears.

So, all of the things that cause you concern are not unique to you. It's simply a matter of degree: your being a child of an alcoholic caused the ordinary difficulties to become more severe.

8. Adult children of alcoholics over-react to changes over which they have no control.

This is very simple to understand. The young child of the alcoholic was not in control. The alcoholic's life was inflicted on him, as was his environment.

In order to survive when growing up, he needed to turn that around. He needed to begin taking charge of his environment. This became very important and remains so. The child of the alcoholic learns to trust himself more than anyone else when it's impossible to rely on someone else's judgment.

As a result, you are very often accused of being controlling, rigid, and lacking in spontaneity. This is probably true. It doesn't come from wanting to do everything your own way. It isn't because you are spoiled or unwilling to listen to other ideas. It comes from the fear that if you are not in charge, if a change is made, abruptly, quickly, and without your being able to participate in it, you will lose control of your life.

When you look back on your reaction and your behavior later, you feel somewhat foolish, but at the time you were simply unable to shift gears.

9. Adult children of alcoholics constantly seek approval and affirmation.

We talk about an external and an internal locus of control. When a child is born, the environment pretty much dictates how he is going to feel about himself. The school, the church, and other people all have influence, but the most important influence is what we call "significant others." In the child's world, this means his parents. So the child begins to believe who he is by the messages that he gets from his parents. And as he gets older, these messages become internalized and contribute significantly to his self-image. The movement is toward the internal locus of control.

The message that you got as a child was very confused. It was not unconditional love. It was not, "I think you're terrific, but I'm not too happy about what you just did." The definitions were not clear and the messages were mixed. "Yes, no, I love you, go away." So you grew up with some confusion about yourself. The affirmations you didn't get on a day-to-day basis as a child, you interpret as negative.

Now, when affirmation is offered, it's very difficult to accept. Accepting the affirmation would be the beginning of changing your self-image.

10. Adult children of alcoholics feel that they are different from other people.

They also assume that in any group of people, everyone else feels comfortable and they are the only ones who feel awkward. This is not peculiar to them. Never, of course, does anyone check it out and find out that each person has his own way of trying not to look awkward. Is that true of you, too?

Interestingly enough, you even feel different in a group of adult children of alcoholics. Feeling different is something you have had with you since childhood and even if the circumstance does not warrant it, the feeling prevails. Other children had an opportunity to be children. You didn't. You were very much concerned with what was going on at home. You could never be completely comfortable playing with other children. You could not be fully there. Your concerns about your home problems clouded everything else in your life.

What happened to you is what happened to the rest of your family. You became isolated. As a result, socializing, being part of any group, became increasingly difficult. You simply did not develop the social skills necessary to feel comfortable or a part of the group.

It is hard for children of alcoholics to believe that they can be accepted because of who they are, and that the acceptance does not have to be earned.

11. Adult children of alcoholics are either super responsible or super irresponsible.

Either you take it all on, or you give it all up. There is no middle ground. You tried to please your parents, doing more and more, or you reached the point where you recognized it didn't matter, so you did nothing. You also did not see a family that cooperated with each other. You didn't have a family that decided on Sunday, "Let's all work in the yard. I will work on this, and you work on that, and then we'll come together."

Not having a sense of being a part of a project, of how to cooperate with other people, and let all the parts come together and become a whole, you either do it all, or you do none of it. You also don't have a good sense of your own limitations. Saying "no" is extraordinarily difficult for you, so you do more and more and more. You do it—(1) because you don't have a realistic sense of your capacity, or (2) because if you say "no" you are afraid that they will find you out. They will find out that you are incompetent. The quality of the job you do does not seem to influence your feelings about yourself. So you take on more and more and more ... until you burn out.

12. Adult children of alcoholics are extremely loyal, even in the face of evidence that the loyalty is undeserved.

The alcoholic home appears to be a very loyal place. Family members hang in long after reasons dictate that they should leave. The so-called "loyalty" is more the result of fear and insecurity than anything else; nevertheless, the behavior that is modeled is one where no one walks away just because the going gets rough. This sense enables the adult child to remain in involvements that are better dissolved.

Since making a friend or developing a relationship is so difficult and so complicated, once the effort has been made, it is permanent. If someone cares enough about you to be your friend, your lover, or your spouse, then you have the obligation to stay with them forever. If you have let them know who you are, if they have discovered who you are and not rejected you, that fact in and of itself is enough to make you sustain the relationship. The fact that they may treat you poorly does not matter. You can rationalize that. Somehow, no matter what they do or say, you can figure out a way to excuse their behavior and find yourself at fault. This reinforces your negative self-image and enables you to stay in the relationship. Your loyalty is unparalleled.

There is also a lot of safety in an established relationship. It is known, and the known is always more secure than the unknown. Change being extremely difficult, you would much prefer to stay with what is.

13. Adult children of alcoholics are impulsive.

They tend to lock themselves into a course of action without giving serious consideration to alternative behaviors or possible consequences. This impulsivity leads to confusion, self-loathing, and loss of control over their environment. In addition, they spend an excessive amount of energy cleaning up the mess.

As a child you could not predict the outcome of any given behavior, so you don't know how to do it now. Also, there was no consistency at home. As a result, you haven't the following framework of "When I behaved impulsively in the past this happened and that happened, and this person reacted in that way." Sometimes it would go O.K., and sometimes it wouldn't.

Essentially, it may not have really mattered. Nor did anyone say to you, "These are the possible consequences of that behavior. Let's talk about other things that you might do."

Alcoholic Parents: Reducing the Impact

By Robert J. Ackerman

Whether you or your spouse have a drinking problem, your children are affected. This is true for your children who are still at home, and for those who are on their own. This article examines recommendations for parents who want to help reduce any detrimental consequences for their children because of exposure to parental alcoholism.

Although sobriety for the alcoholic parent is the best beginning to a solution for alcoholism, not all alcoholics will become sober. Unfortunately, far more continue drinking than those who stop drinking. Additionally, alcoholism recovery is not an instant process. It can take years to overcome denial before seeking help; once in treatment, the treatment itself is time-consuming. To wait for sobriety delays, or totally negates, efforts to help your children. While waiting, marriages can physically or emotionally fall apart, children grow up and leave home, and family members are resigned to quiet desperation. The alternative is to do something—and to do it NOW.

Although desirable, it is not necessary nor a prerequisite for the alcoholic parent to seek help in order to begin helping the children in the family. The alcoholic, as well as the non-alcoholic parent, can help the children. Even though the alcoholic continues drinking, this does not mean that he or she does not want the best for the children. The alcoholic has lost the ability to control his or drinking, but this does not mean that he or she has lost the ability to fell for his or her children. What is in jeopardy for both parents is the ability to openly express these feelings. In the alcoholic family, much energy is absorbed in surviving alcoholic behavior, and there is usually little energy left for other relationships. Because of this survival situation, two necessary ingredients for healthy family relationships become reduced. These are the open expressions of feelings of love, and the energy necessary for positive alternatives.

One of the major problems in alcoholic homes is a lack of energy. Existing energy is usurped to survive the negative influences of alcoholism. This leaves little energy to explore alternatives. Many alcoholic homes are characterized by the family members as being devoid of positive alternatives. The home becomes a "habit cage," and the habit is the repeating of behaviors for survival. There is a major difference between "negative survival" and "positive living." If members of the alcoholic family are going to go beyond mere survival, they must invest new energy and re-direct existing energy twoards positive alternatives in their lives.

One of these alternatives is to openly share feelings and emotions in the home regarding alcoholism and family relationships. However, many feelings, as mentioned earlier, are denied to avoid injury, or they are subjugated for the sake of not rocking the boat. Additionally, with the withdrawing of feelings comes the loneliness of isolation.

You Are Not Alone
Being an alcoholic, or the spouse of an alcoholic, is not an unique numerical situation. There are at least 9.3 to 10 million alcoholics in the United States, and most of these are married. By these statistics, it is obvious that many people are affected by alcoholism, buy why do so many feel alone?

Many of the feelings of loneliness and uniqueness in the alcoholic family come from the attempts to cover up the existence of alcoholism within and outside of the home. A self-imposed silence is used to avoid outside detection, but, unfortunately, it also denies the opportunity for outside help. Within the family, even if members admit and are aware of the alcoholism, they may not be aware of or admit to the need for help, either for themselves or for other members of the family. If you deny that a situation exists or that help is needed, you are not likely to do anything about it. However, living with an alcoholic has very real consequences; the family that denies outwardly will still find itself inwardly covering up the alcoholic behavior. There is little doubt that children in such situations have difficulty understanding when they are asked to cover up for something that they have been told to deny. This is true when children ask, "Where is Dad?" or "What is wrong with Mom?", only to be told that "Nothing is wrong, but do not tell anyone." This parental response is usually an honest attempt by the parent to protect the children. This manner of protection, however, increases isolation within the family, because children are not informed about what is happening in their own family.

On the other hand, the alcoholic or non-alcoholic parent may say, "I've got to protect the children; I don't want them to know what is happening." In this situation, parents are concerned about letting their children know the "real situation," and thus attempt protection. This form of protection seldom works. If your children are capable of observing your behavior, expressions, attitudes, and overall disposition, they kow when you are concerned and anxious. They may not know the exact details regarding the drinking and subsequent behavior, but they know when something is wrong or when one or both parents are upset, drinking, or frustrated. What is needed in this instance is not the wasted attempts at protection, but rather honest efforts to overcome the effects of exposure to alcoholism in your children. Direct your efforts at helping your children to understand and overcome any detrimental consequences of the alcoholic home. Once they are capable of observing the family dynamics, they are beyond protection attempts, and they will need your support in recovering from exposure.

Also, these types of protection attempts may contribute to your feelings of being alone. That is, within your own family, discussion of alcoholism and the sharing of feelings are limited since you are attempting to protect your children by way of silence. Thus, your own efforts are contributing to your feelings of isolation. Your family is a resource for recovery, not a liability contributing to isolation.

Recommendations

Much of what parents can do to assist their children to overcome the consequences of their or thier spouse's alcoholism will depend upon the condition present in each family. The following suggestions are offered for both parents, even though only one may be alcoholic.

- Be flexible regarding the demands that you make on yourself and your children, remembering that problematic situations call for adaptabe measures.
- Try not to isolate yourself and your family from outside interaction or from interaction within your home.
- Do not blame your children for wanting to get help.
- The alcoholic is not to be excused from parenting.
- Do not dwell in the past, learn from it.
- Use alternatives and new endeavors, and not old habits.
- Stop doing what you do **not** do.
- Take care of yourself.
- Get help: NOW!

Do not wait for the right time. It has arrived. Many people feel that they will do something about the family situation when the time is right. Right for what? Postponing help only alows the problems to continue. Additionally, your children need you to act now. If you are concerned about protecting and helping your children, get help for them now. Do not deny their needs because you are not sure of your own.

Hopefully, these recommendations will help to reduce the negative impact on your children of alcoholism. These suggestions, however, are not meant to be used as a vehicle by the alcoholic or non-alchoolic to enable alcoholism to continue. At best, these suggestions can decrease some of the problems, but only sobriety and family growth can overcome all of the problems of alcoholism in the family. Finally, what will really protect your children is the sharing of feelings, concern, and love; the sooner these can be achieved, the sooner yur children can have the best environment to fully live—a healthy family.